HEARTFELT LEADERSHIP

Creating a Culture of Connection

David Larson and Kate Sholonski

Heartfelt Leadership: Creating a Culture of Connection

Copyright © 2014 by Triumph Leadership Group

All rights reserved. No part of this book may be reproduced, stored in a retrieval system or transmitted in any form or by any means electronic, mechanical, photocopying, recording or otherwise without written permission from the authors, except in the case of brief quotations with full credit given to the authors.

Published by

Hell Yeah Publishing
Murrells Inlet, SC 29576

Editor: Jan Birkhofer

Cover Design by: Maria Spencer

Photos by: Bruce Dart

ISBN-13: 978-1501062612
ISBN-10: 1501062611

Printed in the United States of America

Table of Contents

Preface

Staff drama is costing you money.

Negativity is a contagious virus and it is deadly when it takes over a business. What can start out as minor rifts between employees can grow to be a monster that sucks the energy, creativity and subsequently, profits from a business.

You know how it goes. Chronic negativity comes about as a result of backbiting, jealousy, gossip, rumors, co-workers avoiding each other, misplaced anger, frustration, lack of communication, misunderstandings between generations, and day-to-day personality conflicts. The results are varied, such as tardiness, overuse of sick time, diminished productivity, and loss of star players who find the negativity to be intolerable. These are cracks in the foundation of your business that are leaking away your earnings day in and day out.

We think it's a tragedy for business owners to struggle to make money while being confused about how to deal with the staff conflict that is draining their profits. Research has shown that productivity and sales go up 31% or more when staff members are unified as a team as opposed to workers who are unhappy in their work relationships. And with 70% of all workers not liking their jobs, the impact is a serious downward push at the company bottom line.

This book is for business owners and managers who want to take control of their business climate and create a culture of cooperation, collaboration, and cash generation. It's about keeping your workers fully engaged in pursuit of the company mission.

Business leaders who want to bring out the best in their workers to accelerate profits -- or just plain enjoy a business environment free from stress -- will love what they find on these pages. If you are a business owner, team leader or supervisor, you work too hard not to enjoy the process, and you deserve to feel personally fulfilled in all aspects of your life, including your work.

Enlightened bosses who understand the connection between workers liking their jobs and the quality of their production will be inspired by the examples and tools offered here. We're not only going to explain why Heartfelt Leadership works, but also give you strategies for making it real in your workplace.

We're not going to beat around the bush. We're going to make it perfectly clear what to do about staff relationships that give you a headache, and how to handle them with approaches that work to bring about the changes you need.

This isn't fluff. It's not about singing Kum Bah Yah with your staff or doing a company cheer before your employees jump on the phones. It is about recognizing the brilliance in the workers you have, drawing out their highest potential, and creating heartfelt authentic connections that add zeros to your bottom line.

Together, we have decades of personal work experience both in organizations that lost their star players due to negative work environments, as well as in businesses that developed reputations for peak performance and results, and we know what makes the difference between the two.

As a psychologist, David has spent the last 30 years helping resolve every imaginable type of interpersonal conflict, drama, personnel problem and relationship issue leaders face in competing in a dog-eat-dog business world. Kate, once a contributor to a workplace war zone herself, found the secret to profitable relationship building and has gone on to reshape how medical teams deliver exceptional service, re-tool schools and businesses for respect, honesty, and integrity, and show that success can be fun. The suffering is optional.

Join us on the journey of creating the work-life that exceeds your personal expectations, and teaches you how to hold on to your enjoyment of life while making your personal and financial dreams come true.

1

The Contagion Effect

"Our number one priority is company culture. Our whole belief is that if you get the culture right, most of the other stuff like delivering great customer service or building a long-term enduring brand will just happen naturally on its own."

~ Tony Hsieh, CEO Zappos

Your company has a disease. And that disease is spreading straight to your customer. It goes to the core, the very DNA of your organization, and is directly affecting your bottom line.

Here's the good news: This disease acts like a virus, but you get to choose which virus spreads throughout your organization. It can be a one of negativity and drama, or one of positivity and profits. You get to decide.

You know how quickly the contagion elements of a virus such as the flu can spread and how it can create havoc in the workplace as individuals pass it on from one to another, infecting an entire workforce.

The emotional status of each employee is susceptible to being negatively affected in much the same way. High stress environments can be a breeding ground for negative contagions, and if left unchecked, the emotional infection will destroy the work environment similar to a pervasive cancer, gradually consuming the health and profitability of the organization.

Suppose an employee shows up for work feeling agitated from having a tiff with her spouse or children before leaving home, or because she got caught in traffic causing her to be late. She arrives already dampened in spirits, which makes her more likely to infect others with her general sense of dis-ease. She is also more susceptible to being infected by some other negative contagion, whether it comes from another co-worker, a client, or the boss. What may have begun for her as a feeling of annoyance or aggravation can quickly expand into a series of inflammatory negative reactions.

We all know work can be stressful. There are challenges that need to be handled, deadlines to meet, difficult customers who need attention and quotas to hit.

All of these situations create tension, which can leave staff open to the adverse effect of others' moods and actions.

This disease acts like a virus, but you get to choose which virus spreads throughout your organization.

Before you know it, one employee who brought negative energy to work with her is now spreading it by blaming, complaining, avoiding work, being uncooperative on team projects and undermining the success of fellow workers. Moreover, she is often unaware of the turmoil she is creating for the whole team. If the contagion is not identified and treated, a unified team can quickly become a disengaged group.

In my (Kate's) very first job after completing my nurse's training, I was surrounded by multiple sources of the negative contagion. On one of my first assignments in the operating room, I was humiliated and emotionally pummeled when the surgeon chastised me for not knowing an instrument's name. This felt unusually harsh. I vowed to get even. It was easy to do since this O.R. was filled with nurses and surgeons who routinely spread negative emotional contagions. I got sucked into this way of interacting and in a very short time, sold my soul to the negative majority. I abandoned my usual positive demeanor and became one of "them" . . .

The best treatment for the negative contagion is awareness and intervention -- someone calling out the pattern and reversing the energetic direction of conversation or action.

If your team has an alliance developed (as described in chapter 11), there will already be built-in antidotes to negative contagions.

It's also important to know there is a Positive Contagion Effect. This effect occurs when workers are intentionally kind, helpful, respectful, understanding and patient. These attributes and the accompanying energy spread as quickly and powerfully as in the Negative Contagion Effect.

. . . After working in my first O.R. position for two years, I realized I was losing myself as well as my sense of joy and wellbeing by being part of the negative contagion effect. Although much of the time I believed my negativity to be justified, I woke up to see it was only perpetuating

the building of a negative environment. I decided to move on to a new department and practiced being intentional in a positive way with all of my new co-workers.

Positive Contagions occur when a team creates emotional safety and respect for one another in the team. The synergy of a cooperative, positive-moving attitude drives the team to its highest performance, creating a peaceful and smooth-functioning unit for the company along the way. A unified, connected team will not only make your business more fiscally solid, but it will create an environment where you and your employees will enthusiastically look forward to coming to work. Now that's a virus worth spreading!

2

The Importance of Feeling Good

"We can learn through joy or learn through pain – learning through joy is better."

~ David Larson

At times we hear business owners say it's not important to them if their workers are happy; they just want them to be productive! The mutual exclusion of these two ideas is one of the reasons businesses are unnecessarily losing money without their awareness.

We understand that owners, managers, and supervisors want to see every employee showing up at their best, giving their all for the company that employs them. Yet having fun at work is believed by some to impinge on serious commitment, productivity, and a strong work ethic. They may even mistakenly think it wastes time and money.

The truth is what really hurts the bottom line is the impact of a negative work environment.

Here's an example:

According to the Integrated Benefits Institute, sick time costs United States businesses $576 billion a year. [1]

What do you think the first thing workers do if they are not happy at work? They call in sick! Not only are the businesses paying their employees for time not worked, but staff replacement alone costs them billions of dollars annually just to keep their organizations from grinding to a halt when workers are gone. [2]

It's important for business leaders to stop the drain of losing money due to staff conflict, drama, work dissention, and inefficiencies in performance. The drain shows up not only as overused sick time, but also as gossip and unhealthy cliques that create chronic staff tension. Additionally, it appears as negativity in employee attitudes and time wasted when they are distracted by anger, frustration, or fear involving their coworkers or boss. All of this is costly to your business, and it's just not necessary.

Room for Joy

We have worked on teams that were fun loving, as well as with teams that were grim and cutthroat in their interactions. Without a doubt, the teams that held a high value around team connectedness and spirited engagement not only had more enjoyable work environments, but also were more efficient and productive in their work.

Supporting joy in the workplace produces greater camaraderie where employees sincerely care about their co-workers and seek to help one another when the going gets tough. Employee turnover stress costs American businesses about 150% or more of an annual salary for each replacement in a professional role. This cost includes lost knowledge, lost work while a position is vacant, and overworked remaining staff. There are also costs of advertising and recruiting expenses, as well as the loss of productivity during interviewing and training each new employee. For lower-cost employees, the tab runs about $3,500.00 to replace one $8.00 per hour employee when all costs were considered. [3] In a joyful work environment, employee turnover is reduced, since the workplace climate attracts employees to come in to work instead of tempting them to stay home.

Employers who see their workers as more than just machines that punch clocks have heart-to-heart connections with them, enhancing the relationships that bring reduced stress and maximum performance from everyone. Joy, compassion, fun, understanding and sincere connection produce healthier and more productive team relationships.

The Happiness Factor

Sales go up 37%. There is less burnout, less turnover, more resilience, and greater employee retention.

Harvard scientist Shawn Anchor [4] has been studying the link between happiness and success for many years. He has studied workers in 45 countries, examining every conceivable factor that contributes to success.

According to Anchor, most people mistakenly believe that hard work leads to more success, and then happiness follows. Their perception looks like this:

Hard Work → Success → Happiness

What Anchor found in his research is that this philosophy is scientifically backward. What he observed was the more efficient path was that if you can achieve happiness first, happiness leads to *even better* performance, which then leads to more success. We have found this to be true.

Here's how it really works:

Happiness → Hard Work → More Success

Measures of success, when the value of happiness was acknowledged, were astonishing. Anchor reports that workers are 31% more productive when they are happy than if they are negative, neutral, or stressed. Sales go up 37%. There is less burnout, less turnover, more resilience, and greater employee retention. They have more energy, are more creative, and act more intelligently. "Every single business outcome improves," says Anchor. One of the chemicals in the brain that contributes to our happiness – dopamine - floods receptors to turn on the learning centers of the brain, making workers more productive in every way. This isn't wishful thinking. This is science.

When working with a team of engineers, one gentleman spoke clearly to this issue. "When I wake up excited to go to work, I arrive in stride, already on beat! When I have to force myself to go, it takes me hours to get up to speed."

Imagine if there was room for feeling good in every group, on every team, in every home, and in every business. In this type of environment, problems are solved more quickly, people are more collaborative and communicative, and cooperation is the norm. That combination is not only a successful one for making money for the business, but it is paving a positive track for others to follow. That is effective leadership.

If you are one of those who has believed that is doesn't matter if your workers are happy, we challenge you to rethink this. What could you do with 37% more revenue?

3

Fear is the Source of All Conflict

"People fail to get along because they fear each other; they fear each other because they don't know each other; they don't know each other because they have not communicated with each other."

~ Rev. Martin Luther King

If you look up "emotions" on your favorite browser, you will find lists of dozens of emotional states, everything from anger and anxiety to affection and amusement. Many people reduce this assortment of more than 60 emotions into four categories: mad, sad, glad, and scared. Frustration is a form of "mad," for example, and worry is a form of "scared." All emotions can fit into the four categories of mad, sad, glad, and scared.

A Course in Miracles [5] further reduces the number of emotions to two: Love and Fear. We have found this to be extremely practical in helping people handle emotions, which humans bring to work every day.

We have noticed that every interpersonal conflict arising in a work setting can be traced back to fear. For example, when workers are jealous of one another, they are afraid of something – that a co-worker has what they can't have or that they won't be able to obtain. When people are anxious, they are afraid something is out of their control that may eventually hurt them. When they are irritated (a form of anger or "mad"), they are scared someone is stealing their peace or are afraid of being controlled. Emotional upsets are based in fear.

Fears are at the basis of negative behaviors and attitudes, as well. Manipulation and stubbornness come from fear of losing control. Gossip, backbiting, yelling, and cruelty also come from fear, each being an expression of not feeling at peace within one's self.

It is important for us as leaders to understand the emotions of our employees in order to make appropriate and effective interventions in changing behaviors that can mar a workplace culture and interrupt otherwise efficient production.

The first question for us to ponder when assessing what's going on in a negative environment, is "What is (that person) afraid of?"

When you are aware of what the people you are responsible for are fearing, it gives you great power to intervene in a way that not only stops the negative interactions in their tracks, but allows you to change the dynamic permanently.

In short, workers that feel good produce the most.

Not only does every interpersonal negative interaction arise from fear, but every negative emotion can be mitigated by love. When someone's fear is acknowledged and taken care of, they return to their center and balance, and to an optimum state of service and productivity. No longer are they distracted by their emotional response to whatever is going on, but can re-focus and get back to work in a way that represents an expression of their highest potential. In short, workers that feel good produce the most. Leaders who ignore this fact lose the most.

Example 1:

Recently, in listening to the stories shared by one of our clients, we noticed that every complaint he had regarding the day-to-day running of the business revolved around mistakes others were making. Even when directly asked what role he played in the dramas or inefficient activities, he was unable to see that he may also be making errors in judgment.

This employee tends to be anxious and hypersensitive about following rules and protocol, and the thought of changing his work routines tends to frighten him. His determination to be "right" struck us as being reflective of his own fear of being "wrong."

Our goal in coaching him was to melt down the barrier that protects his *rightness*. What we wanted for him was to respect and love himself enough that he could listen to his co-worker's ideas openly without needing to judge them, and work with them in solving problems.

We could see that until he let go of this insecurity, his fear would continue to keep him hiding behind the wall he had built in his mind and around his heart. It would keep him from understanding that giving up his need to be right would actually give him the freedom and peace he seeks.

We supported him with love, urging him to peek through the chinks in his fearful wall, trusting that self-love will always keep him safe.

Example 2:

Suppose you gave a raise to one of your staff, Ron, and someone else in the department, Susan, begrudges it. Susan's resentment can lead to inefficiency at best, or sabotage of work projects at worst. As a leader, you know this resentment has at its source a fear. For Susan, it may be a fear that a raise is not forthcoming for herself, or that someone else is getting ahead of her professionally. Perhaps it stimulates her insecurities of not measuring up, or about the quality of her own performance.

After recognizing the fear is at the source of Susan's negative attitude and behavior, addressing the fear moves Susan out of her stuck place and back into a cooperative frame of mind on the team. It might transpire something like this:

Calling Susan into your office, you say, "You may have heard that Ron received a raise this week for his exceptional performance over the last six months. I am hoping to give you a raise as well in the future, and this is what I would like to see from you..."

You go on to explain what behaviors and performance factors will earn her a raise, setting up the clarity she needs to know about how to improve her own performance that would result in that raise. This calms her fear that she is missing out. She is likely to feel valued that you spoke with her and gave her clear information that would empower her to earn her own raise. You also provided a structure for her to let go of her resentment. And, to top it all off, you have eliminated any false assumptions she may have believed to be true about you, Ron, or the workplace that would have continued to feed her fears. All of this happened because you responded to her fear in a caring and direct fashion.

Triumph Geography

Imagine at any given moment you reside in one of two emotional lands. One is the Land of Love, and the other is the Land of Fear.

The Land of Love is where you feel your best. You feel secure and therefore interact with others in a way that promotes confidence. You have respect for yourself and everyone else. You are aligned with your highest self and all of the gifts that come with it, such as compassion for yourself and others, patience, understanding, cooperation, sensitivity, collaboration, alignment, forgiveness, peace and joy.

When you are in the Land of Love, you feel good. When you feel good, you treat others and yourself in a positive and respectful way.

When you are spending most of your time in the Land of Love, you will be energized and will have a positive viewpoint on your life and work. You are not easily pulled into a negative state of mind and are not easily offended, since you are aware of how others are simply projecting their fears on you.

You can probably imagine how much more work would get done in business, families and even the government, if people hung out in the Land of Love on a regular basis.

The alternative to the Land of Love is the Land of Fear. In this Land, you will be feeling negative emotions like anger, jealousy and resentment. The expected results of hanging out in the Land of Fear would be a lack of trust of others, being negatively judgmental and generally defensive. It is often difficult for some people to see a connection between these less pleasing emotions and fear itself, yet we know that all of the negative emotions have at their source some sort of fear.

When you consider several people in a group, family or workplace all inhabiting the Land of Fear at the same time, you can probably imagine the disagreements, lack of cooperation, and messes that would result, all of which have at their origin some level of misunderstanding.

The reason these messes are a natural outcome is that people in the Land of Fear are out of alignment with their natural gifts, so the power of their positive impact on those around them will be compromised. In fact, not being aware of one's fear can be the quickest way to kill the energy and enthusiasm that is needed for a team's top performance.

*****

We once attended a training seminar where well-intentioned workshop leaders used fear as their major motivator. They were adamant about focusing on what we did wrong, and emphasized it by calling us names and blaming us for not understanding the concepts. Either purposely or by accident, they would leave out instructions about what was expected of us, which left plenty of room for them to be disappointed in our performance. They encouraged us to ask questions, yet when we did so, we were chastised for asking the wrong questions.

The impact of this form of leadership actually undermined our learning and mastery. Our natural creativity disappeared. We struggled to recover our confidence. We felt confused and lost, all signs of being in the Land of Fear. We watched some of our fellow students totally freeze, unable to share their views in fear of being knocked down again. The trainers seemed to believe that if they could motivate us to feel bad about ourselves, it would provide the best inspiration to improve. They had no idea that they were in reality creating our poor performance by keeping us in constant fear of more criticism.

Have you ever experienced something like this?

We recommend instead creating an atmosphere of support and unconditional acceptance. We have found that people, regardless of their age, background or work experience, are drawn to bringing their best selves forward when they are acknowledged for what they do well.

As you practice catching your employees or co-workers in the act of doing something right, they will more likely remain positively focused and will continue to make progress. When you are seen as one who believes in their potential, trust grows, and they will then be better able to hear how they can improve.

This approach feels good to the ones you are trying to influence, and they are motivated to excel because they want to continue to feel good. Isn't that what we all want anyway? We will do virtually anything, including spending lots of money, taking exotic vacations, or seeking fame and fortune, just so we can feel good. Instead, we recommend capitalizing on this phenomenon to everyone's advantage in the work environment by using the most powerful motivation possible - supporting people in feeling good - to bring out top performance.

4

The Most Powerful Transformative Agent in the World

"Love and compassion for your team is more motivating than trying to beat the opponent."

~ Bobby Bowden, Florida State Seminoles

Love is not a dirty four-letter word.

We believe in love, because love creates the most miracles. It changes lives most profoundly. It's what we've seen prevents the most suicides, saves the most marriages, transforms the most depression, dissolves the most anxiety, changes the most bullies, and helps the most-wounded recover.

Love is highly correlated with peace, life satisfaction, and living a life of meaning. It breeds healthy bodies and healthy emotions, contributes to low stress, and is energizing. It gets people out of bed in the morning, feeds the passions of life, and as we shall see, helps people make more money.

Love acknowledges that people always do their best in the moment. As they gain new tools, new insights, new support, new strategies, and new opportunities, they can perform even better. The opposite - shaming, blaming, yelling, humiliating, and embarrassing - doesn't bring out the best in people. Teaching people to love and respect themselves, give up the anger and resentment that holds them back, and making sure they get what they need to do their best – this is when the miracles happen.

Coaches and Business Leaders Know It

We are fans of John Wooden, the six-time national college coach of the year, who led his team to 12 NCAA championships at UCLA, and Pat Summit of the University of TN, the most successful women's basketball coach in history. They cited the key elements that brought out the best in their teams to be "caring, love, balance, and gentleness." [6] Both of these Hall of Famers saw their role as being an example of respectful relationships, dealing with their players as human beings, and caring about the whole of their lives, not just what they do on the court. Wooden further clarifies, "What you are as a person is far more important than what you are as a basketball player." [7] What is true for Wooden's teams is also true for your team. Developing your team members into the best people they can be creates the best performers on the job.

Personal relationships are the cornerstone of companies, according to Tony Hsieh of Zappos. "It's important that managers and supervisors get to know their employees on a personal basis. The results have been better communication between employees, relationships are better, people are willing to do favors for each other, and higher levels of trust are established." [8]

As Bobby Bowden states in the opening quote of this chapter, we get the most mileage from our efforts when we focus on unifying our teams. This is a "win-win" approach. Learning to respect those around us is far more productive in moving us forward than the "win-lose" mindset of trying to "beat out" others.

You likely want to create a culture in your organization like Bert Jacobs has at the "Life is Good" company. They adopted a phrase there that reflects their positivity and their commitment. They don't have to or need to do anything. They "get to" serve. They "get to" work. They "get to" appreciate life. They "get to" choose a positive attitude. They don't have 4,500 stores in 30 countries because they force, coerce, threaten, or manipulate anyone to do anything. They're a multi-million dollar company because they love going to work where they "get to" provide excellent customer service.

Physical Healers Know It

Dr. Bernie Siegel, author of *Love, Medicine, and Miracles*, is well known for his work in healing, particularly self-healing and the power of love to heal. He reports that a Harvard study determined students who described their parents as unloving suffered a major illness by midlife three times more often than those who felt loved by their parents.   It has also been shown that cancer patients who attend support groups live, on the average, twice as long after their diagnosis as those who don't have that support. [9]   Lack of the presence of love promotes illness, and presence of love extends life.

The same principle applies in the work environment. It's clear that in the workplace, loving support creates positive energy; verbal attack takes it away. Caring brings out a person's highest potential; put-downs drain motivation and create anxiety that inhibits production.

Chunyi Lin, creator of Spring Forest Qigong, who has trained more than 200,000 students in the art of healing, repeats again and again, *the most powerful element of physical healing is love.* [10]   This love energy is frequently found to restore health and vibrancy in numerous unhealthy conditions such as infections, high cholesterol, cancer, burn injuries, and internal bleeding. [11]

Greg Gerber, MD, the Chief of Internal Medicine at SW Memorial Hospital, Houston, Texas reports the benefits of Chunyi Lin's approach "are fantastic--absolutely remarkable. Diabetes, glucose control, hypertension--I've seen some folks reversing other longer-standing arthritis--all of these are on the list of what I've seen in my clinical practice being reversed." [12]

Medical expert Dr. Bill Manahan, of the University of Minnesota Medical School cannot be more enthusiastic about the power of love in Chunyi Lin's methods. "Spring Forest Qigong is going to revolutionize the manner in which we look at healing . . . I would place qigong equal in importance to the incredible discoveries in the forties called antibiotics and in the fifties called immunizations." [13]

Physical healing manifests from the power of love. Writes Vironika Tugaleva, "Love is not the opposite of power. Love IS power. Love is the strongest power there is." [14]

Winners of All Ages Know It

The process of love works for young people, as well as adults. Kate brought to the world a wonderful witness to the power of love to transform human beings into bundles of life-changing energy. She did it with teenagers by helping them see their greatness within.

Kate gathered diverse high school students into small groups for the purpose of developing unconditional respect for their peers. The geeks, the athletes, the outcasts, the students with the highest GPAs, and those who struggled academically all signed on with the agreement that they would treat each other as equals. Kate helped them to recognize what united them, not what separated them. Through weekly meetings with creative games and openhearted, honest discussions, she saw hearts soften and love and kindness become the norm. The non-judgmental supportive atmosphere she created helped students turn confusion into clarity, and conflict into understanding. Kate could see who they were, and she pointed them to see it in themselves until they could no longer deny their internal greatness. The result was once they found love for themselves, they also found it for one another. Bullies ceased to be bullies, and non-aggressive students learned to stop the bullying behavior of others. Students learned how not to be pulled down by the negativity of others. Grades improved. Confidence blossomed. Some students created powerful programs to help younger students overcome their limitations. Some went on to spread empowering principles of respectful relationships through programs developed on their college campuses. Kate's program, *Project: Inside Out,* became a high school leadership program that helped kids of all circumstances become their best, and share their best with the world in need. Love transforms.

How could your workers be transformed by honoring their uniqueness, caring about their challenges, and loving them into greatness? How would it affect your bottom line?

A rose blooms most beautifully, not by trying to pry it open by force, but by putting it in a warm cup of water, where it will naturally open to display its magnificent beauty. Trying to force others to change brings resistance. Nurturing facilitates cooperation. We all want our coworkers to relax and bring their best selves forward, not shrink in fear that we'll point out again how they're not good enough.

Foster Cooperation, Not Resistance

We sometimes do an exercise in our workshops that helps people understand this point. Standing divided into pairs, one person holds his hands up palms outward in front of him. The other person is instructed to push against his partner's hands.

They never say "have to" or "need to." They only say, "Get to."

Instinctively, almost automatically, the first person, feeling pressure

34

against his hands, pushes back. It's a self-preservation defense to avoid being thrown off balance or overcome by an outside force.

The same thing happens psychologically when someone is forceful, overbearing, critical or intimidating. There is a natural resistance that shows up whenever people feel like they're being pressured to do something they don't understand or causes them to feel threatened. This resistance is definitely not what we want to foster in our employees.

As leaders, we do not want those we're responsible for to resist us; we want them to cooperate and be encouraged to move forward with their responsibilities.

Marianne Williamson, author of "A Return to Love," speaks well to this issue: "When we are shaking a finger at someone, figuratively or literally, we are not more apt to correct his wrongful behavior. Treating someone with compassion and forgiveness is much more likely to elicit a healed response. People are less likely to be defensive, and more likely to be open to correction." [15]

The exemplary coaches mentioned earlier in this chapter knew how important it was to focus on the positive in showing people how to get better. They seldom spent time pounding into their players how badly they'd done. They focused not on what was poorly executed, but on what needed to be done well.

As hockey great Wayne Gretzky said, "I always skate to where the puck is going, not where it's been." [16]

Isn't this where you want to point your workers? You don't emphasize their mistakes of the past, but rather the results you want to see in the future. Isn't it nice to know you can not only capitalize on the genius your employees bring with them to the job, but can also nurture them to even more greatness under your influence?

If love can produce winning sports teams, heal wounded souls, and create healthy bodies, it can produce winning workgroups and business success.

You don't have to talk about love in your workplace to bring your environment to its maximum performance level, but you do have to *be* it and *show* it.

Because you want a work culture that meets and exceeds your expectations, you foster a climate where people know they're cared about, supported, and loved. They know they 'get to' come to work, because they feel good working in your company. Your workers feel free to laugh in the office, and you laugh yourself - all the way to the bank!

5

Essence Leadership

"Great leaders honestly care about those they lead. Their egos have nothing to prove."

~ Kate Sholonski

If you have been a member of the work force, or been on sports teams, committees or in clubs, you have most likely experienced the stark difference between an Essence Leader and an Ego Leader.

The easiest way to identify if a leader leads with their *Ego* or *Essence*, is to notice how you feel in their presence. If you feel comfortable to be yourself and notice they tend to bring out your best, you are in the presence of an *Essence Leader.* [17]

If you tend to be a bit on edge, defensive and likely fearful of making a mistake or being emotionally hurt, an *Ego Leader* is likely to be the one in charge.

The Ego Leader operates from fear and stimulates the same reaction in others. Although ego-driven leaders may appear to be very confident, somewhere within them they doubt their authentic in-born value. They aren't living up to their innate gifts and tend to try hard to prove to you they are worthy of your respect and attention. They may also be forceful or loud, or in some cases quiet, yet passive-aggressive in their behaviors. Although ego leaders may not be aware of any sense of lack within themselves, their impact on others will often be similar to bullies on the playground who believe they must use force to prove they are better than you.

Says Deepak Chopra, "The Ego, however, is not who you really are. The ego is your self-image; it is your social mask; it is the role you are playing. Your social mask thrives on approval. It wants control . . . because it lives in fear." [18]

While Ego Leaders tend to spend a lot of time in the Land of Fear, Essence Leaders will operate from the Land of Love. They do this instinctively because they know that love is a natural part of who they are, and they recognize that drawing out the best performances in others means helping their workers see the best in themselves.

It is this authentic compilation of gifts that makes every person unique. When an individual knows and trusts all the gifts that come with who they are, they have nothing to fear. As a result they will naturally elicit a positive response from others since it is their mission to do so.

"Essence leadership is designed to call forth the best in people by focusing on who they are as a foundation for what they do. They harvest the goodness of people and emphasize their uniqueness and their individuality." [19]

Essence leaders don't have a need to convince or prove anything. They respect themselves and are not afraid to make a mistake. They often radiate a calmness that puts others at ease, so their workers can also better work from their essence.

At other times we will observe Essence Leaders to have a natural expression of vitality and enthusiasm. Essence leaders spend very little time worrying. They handle stress well, and they have a way of relieving the stress of others rather than adding to it.

Please note the chart below as a quick reference for evaluating whether you or someone else you know tends toward Ego or Essence in their leadership style.

Ego Leaders	Essence Leaders
Work stressed	Work actively but relaxed
Try hard	Simply do their best
Act but don't feel 'Good Enough'	Share gifts/skills with joy
Are often grumpy or harsh	Often smile and enjoy their work
Yell, manipulate, or accuse	State clearly without accusation
Defend, judge, criticize	Are compassionate, patient, respectful
Are often angry, anxious or hurt	Are seldom angry, anxious, hurt
Have difficulty trusting staff	Trust easily with confidence
Believe someone has to be blamed	Believe no one has to be blamed
Compare workers	Appreciate the gifts of each worker
Hold grudges; stay stuck	Forgive easily; move forward
See self as superior	See self as equal
Hold accountable with harshness	Hold accountable with support
Motivate through fear	Motivate through positive caring

*****

I (Kate) have personally been under the influence of both Ego and Essence leaders, and can clearly see the impact each has had on my professional development.

As a young nursing student, I was very fortunate to train under the direction of a wonderful Essence Leader. Miss Konecke was a single lady, probably in her early fifties and treated everyone, including her patients, with complete love and respect. She was also a stickler about technique and would not let any of her students get away with "slip-shod" work, as she called it, when it came to our nursing care. She was personally committed to training top-notch nurses, and she did.

Miss Konecke brought out the best in each of us since she didn't beat us down, causing us to doubt ourselves. She expected the best from us and managed to provide the perfect combination of loving care and clear expectations in expressing what she wanted to see in our performance. The result was that we all worked very hard to meet her expectations. When we did a good job, she let us know. When we missed the mark, she also let us know, but she had a way of correcting us that called us forth to do better rather than feel embarrassed or humiliated. We all knew she sincerely cared about us, both personally and professionally. Miss Konecke's influence on my life was so powerful, I still think of her impact today, forty-three years later.

Soon after this experience with an Essence Leader, I took my first job as an operating room nurse. Although I didn't

40

know it at the time, my supervisor was definitely an Ego Leader. She ran the O.R. like a drill sergeant and spoke to her nurses as if we were recruits in Army boot camp. Unlike Miss Konecke, Mrs. Warner did not inspire her team to do great work. Instead, she created an environment where we preferred to stay under the radar, since we feared her wrath. We didn't trust her. We avoided her as much as possible and never volunteered to be in a situation that might backfire and cause us to be openly reprimanded. She stifled our creativity and we avoided learning the more challenging skills because we were in fear of making a mistake. She put a lid on our natural ability to learn and grow into being better nurses.

When we refer to *Essence*, we mean the deep truth or spiritual make-up of a person.

Mrs. Warner's leadership had the opposite effect on my fellow nurses and me as Miss Konecke's did. Instead of being dedicated followers, we were fearful, resistant and reactive. In looking back now, I understand why. There was no connection or trust. Working under this ego leader tended to bring out the worst of our team, rather than the best. We were not inspired or committed to do our finest work since it didn't seem as though anyone really cared. The old adage applies here:

"People don't care about how much you know until they know how much you care." [20]

41

The following story is an example of a common experience we see that discourages employees from doing their best for the company.

Tim shared with us an incident where he was called out and yelled at by his boss in front of fellow staff members. The reason for this reprimand was based on assumptions, not facts, which made the demonstration even harder to justify or understand. The truth is, even if our client had made the error, tearing him down in front of others did not correct it, nor was it likely to prevent future infractions. Tim related his embarrassment and frustration to us, and confessed that he wasn't sure how much more he could take, indicating that he was thinking about looking elsewhere for work.

His departure would be a rough one for the company, since his contributions and the responsibility he held were significant.

The trickle-down effect of this one act of disrespect affected the whole team. When co-workers saw Tim being cut down based on assumptions they knew were not true, their own concern for receiving the same treatment increased.

As fear goes up, trust in the boss goes down, as does worker performance. Remember, 70% of workers don't like their bosses. And it's hard to give your best for someone you don't respect. Even less fortunate in this situation is that this client was the glue that held this team together. Losing him could cause this small company to fall apart like a house of cards. The truth spoken by Tony Hsieh of Zappos rang true in Tim's experience:

"People don't leave companies; they leave their managers." [21]

*****

The type of situation described above is like a time bomb and it needs to be handled delicately and expeditiously. The longer the pattern of disrespectful treatment goes on, the greater the fear will be within the team. When a team is working under a cloud of fear, there will be a loss of confidence, less creativity, and subsequently less productivity.

We've heard it said, "Suicide is murder, but it's the survivors who get the bullet." Ego Leaders have a similar impact. They take out their fear on their employees, but it's the business that takes the hit.

The good news for ego leaders is that they, too, have an essence. Connecting them to that essence and practicing leading from there is just the ticket that can save workplaces like Tim's from disintegrating.

Essence leaders lead with the heart, and heart-felt leadership is the most effective way we know to catalyze the employee performance that takes businesses to the top.

6

The Power of the Team

"It's all about the teamwork, not the stars."

~Lute Olsen, University of Arizona super-coach

Respect Leads the Way

In this day and age, macho is out; finesse is in. It used to be enough just to scare employees into submission, but those days are over. And there's a reason for that. It just doesn't work very well.

We know now that 75% of success is due to positive attitude, adequate support, and seeing stress as a challenge, not a threat. [22] Threats are for leaders who don't know what else to do and haven't learned true leadership. People want to be successful, and good leaders help their team members to excel and bring out their best. They don't put them down or try to force them into obedience. It doesn't work in personal relationships, and it doesn't work in business.

Good leaders don't intimidate. Good leaders don't embarrass. Good leaders don't humiliate.

Good leaders inspire. Good leaders see the best in their players, whether they're players on the ball field or players in the sales field. They bring it out with tools of positivity, including encouragement, unconditional support and challenges to play even bigger. They see what their workers are capable of before the workers see it in themselves, and they don't try to hammer it out of them, they lead them to it.

*****

A few weeks into his new management position, Gary noticed staff sick-time was averaging 10-11 days per person, twice what would typically be expected. Without blame or attack, Gary called a meeting.

"I've been noticing these figures of sick time used this past year. Do you think they are accurate?" he asked. After receiving an affirmative reply from the people in the room, he explained that 5-6 days per person would be a typical average for use of sick time in a year.

Gary continued, "Is there anything going on in the office climate that is stressful and affecting the sick time requests?"

There was none that the staff could identify.

"Any ergonomic issues that might be aggravating health conditions for anyone?"

Once again, it was acknowledged no problems existed.

"Well, let's watch this a little closer and see if we can figure out what's happening that these sick days are needed," said Gary. "We want to get to the bottom of whatever we can do to keep everyone as healthy as possible."

*****

Since that discussion, the issue of overused sick time is no longer an issue.

46

How could something so simple and straightforward work? Without yelling, condemning, threatening, or blaming, Gary turned an awareness into a solved problem.

Had this leader approached the staff with, "Sick time is way too high for this group! You guys need to knock it off!" he would have put them on the defensive. They would have backed away emotionally and energetically, trying to figure out phony excuses and how not to anger their new boss in the future. They would have expended energy figuring out how to cover up their tracks and not draw future tongue-lashings. Gary would have missed the opportunity to assess whether his people needed equipment replaced, or if something in the work environment was causing health problems, or whether there was a problem in his system that was contributing to overuse of sick time.

Clearly, a non-blaming, compassionate, concerned-for-their-well-being approach saved his department thousands of dollars by asking a few simple questions in a way that did not judge or degrade his workers. This is effective leadership. This is the power of respect for self and others in the workplace. It saves money at the bottom line. It builds and strengthens the relationship between boss and employees. And it keeps people in their most creative and positive space to do their best job.

*****

Trust

The High Wire

As part of a leadership training program years ago, I (David) was paired with a partner for an exercise that taught me something I will never forget. We were led to a wooded area where a tightrope was stretched about 40 feet between two trees, 15 feet in the air. We were told that we had five minutes to come up with a topic on which to speak, and that we would then spontaneously give that speech while walking across the high wire.

The challenge seemed enormous. There were no resources available to do research and little time to plan. We were given a physical challenge to do something neither my partner nor I had done before, while delivering a knockout presentation from the air!

If we had allowed fear to take over, we would not only have put ourselves in physical danger, but it would have created a tension between us that would have destroyed our ability to collaborate delivering a speech under very challenging circumstances.

As we approached the tree to get on the high wire, it became extremely obvious to me that without trust, we had nothing. We had to trust the wire would hold us. We had to trust our bodies would be strong enough and our balance good enough to keep us upright on the wire. We had to trust each other that we would be doing our very best in presenting. There was no room for doubt. There was only room for complete focus. There could be no arguing or disagreeing. There simply was no time for that. We were called forth to support each other both physically and emotionally, while delivering a speech for which neither of us had prepared. This required each of us to add coactively and supportively to whatever came out of our partner's mouth, to deliver coherently and entertainingly a presentation while physically doing the unimaginable.

We were so focused on doing our job that we were halfway across the abyss below us before I realized what we were doing was impossible. As soon as the negative thought entered my mind that we could not possibly be accomplishing this feat, I lost my balance, and we tumbled into the air, supported, of course, by a belay team, who by doing their jobs, allowed us to land safely on the ground.

*****

Have you ever been faced with a situation that you thought was impossible to complete successfully, and self-doubt kept you from even trying? Have you ever been in a situation that was so urgent or so pressured by timelines or importance that you knew you had to do it right the first time – that there was no room for mistakes? Were you able to draw on the resources within yourself, and to ask for and depend on help from others when the stakes were high?

In many businesses, the stakes are high every day. What is needed is focus, collaboration, mutual support and trust. Without these elements, the project is doomed to failure.

Whether a work-related task is urgent or is one that

happens every day, wouldn't you want to know you could count on your team to be there for you, to insure you have everything you need to do a fantastic job?

Unity

You may have heard of the 1970 tragedy when a plane carrying Marshall University's football team veered off its planned route and crashed into the ground a few miles short of its intended landing site. Everyone on board the plane was killed – 46 players and coaches, plus fans, alumni, community supporters & crew. The story was recalled in a 2006 movie called "We Are Marshall."

In the grief of such an unspeakable loss, the challenge of re-building a college football team from scratch seemed nearly insurmountable. The remaining undergraduate players were ineligible to play on the varsity squad. Convincing potential newbies to join a team of sparsely trained rookies, doomed to be trampled on by the more experienced teams, was not exactly an attraction for drawing new students to their program. Many thought the school should just hang it up . . . EXCEPT for a newly hired athletic director and a 3rd round unknown coach named Jack Lengyel.

Lengyel had a vision that could not be contained, that called forth the best in himself and others. He overcame mountains of obstacles, visiting high school football players himself and asking them to join his team. Lengyel put together a squad of walk-ons, freshmen, ex-servicemen, three basketball players and a kicker from the soccer team. Lengyel asked for help from rival coaches, some of which shared playbook secrets to help him rebuild his team. He literally raised a football team out of ashes.

Although the road was long, since rebuilding the squad in 1971, Marshall posted a streak of 21 straight winning seasons, won three conference championships, and produced 35 NFL players.

In an interview much later in Lengyel's career, he was asked his secret to success, and he said this:

"Team effort is what counts . . . you can accomplish anything if you're united." [23]

Do you feel like you sometimes face unbearable odds in your business? Do you sometimes feel you want to give up, not seeing the light of day at the end of the road? Do you have a rag-tag team that seems impossible to get to work together?

There is no substitute for unity. Your team must function like a well-tuned engine in order for them to exceed your expectations. You want your profit margin climbing through a dedicated group that excels in the face of challenges. You need a TEAM, a *unified* TEAM.

Collaboration

Often in our work with teams, we have the opportunity to return for follow- up training. In these trainings, we get to see what changes have occurred in their day-to-day work routines and relationships since our last visit.

*****

During a two-day leadership training at a teachers' conference, we first focused on the importance of self-care, self-compassion and self-forgiveness. At first it was challenging for this group to see themselves in such a vulnerable way. After some engaging exercises, however, they loosened up and got comfortable with the idea that it was not only okay for them to be kind to themselves in thought and actions, it was imperative. What they learned was how they felt in any given moment influenced how they treated others and how well they connected with their students.

The second day of our training was focused on professional skills where they learned principles and tools they could practice in their daily routines that would create a network of trust and connectedness, rather than one of separateness.

At the completion of our time with this group, they made firm commitments to themselves and to their co-workers to be more collaborative, cooperative and overall, more positive. Also exciting was that they spontaneously created a plan to keep their enthusiasm alive.

Fast forward . . . One Year Later . . .

When we returned the following year, we heard many success stories of how they not only maintained their positive approach, but they expanded it with a variety of actions, including holding one another accountable on practices of self-care. Since they were all committed to creating a less toxic work environment, and believed success for the group meant that they would each hold a vital part in creating a more solid team, they made a special effort to look out for one another.

A heart-warming part of their story was that their overall attitude about going to work improved. Since they knew their co-workers had their backs no matter what showed up, they felt more confident in knowing they could meet any challenge. One teacher told us, "In the past, it felt like when I went to work everyday I was alone on an island, and now I feel as if I am a vital part of a community."

What was clearly evidenced to us in watching the expansion of connectedness within this team was that humans need each other to grow. Although as individuals we each have something great to contribute to a team, it is mutual support, connection and shared desire that sets some teams apart as exceptional, while the ones that struggle are a team in name only.

Recovering From Mistakes

Forgiveness is a word that either inspires people or freaks them out. Some say it's a concept that doesn't belong in a business book. We disagree.

Forgiveness is about releasing mistakes. It's about choosing to focus on desired behavior, not lamenting undesired behavior. Forgiveness means not holding onto the past. It's capturing the energy you have to solve problems in the present.

Forgiveness is *letting go*. It's understanding that the past can't be changed, nor do you need it to. The present is the only time you have. You can only accomplish things "*now,*" not "before," or "yesterday," or "last week." Think of how much money is wasted in concentrating our energy somewhere else besides the present, which is the only place *anything* positive can happen.

In the workplace, people will make mistakes. We are not advocating overlooking blunders. We're not recommending you ignore steps to help someone improve, or pretend something didn't happen. What we want to do is remind you that instilling guilt is a very poor motivator, and is a waste of time for you and your employees. We recall the past in a useful way only if it helps us zero in on what we want to do differently in the present and future. We can squander valuable time focusing on what can't be changed, when what is more helpful is focusing on what needs to be done from the present moment forward.

You already know that feeling bad yields poorer performance. Feeling good takes people to the top of their game. When you focus on what has been done wrong, both you and your employees are drained of energy, making you both weaker and less productive.

Many leaders think that by making employees feel bad it will motivate them to better behavior. What will motivate your workers more is when they know their missteps did not derail you. What energizes *them* for you is helping them to let go and get re-focused. What your employees

Forgiveness is *letting go.*

need is knowing you are still fully in their corner, and invested in quickly returning them to a positive frame of mind in order to be of better service to your company.

Do you hold people accountable? Yes. Do you fire people when they aren't doing the job? Yes. Can you take the time to grieve the loss that has occurred? Yes. Does that mean you focus on it? No. Your time is too valuable for that. Making money requires that you always move forward and resist getting stuck in an occurrence that can't be changed. The most important question you should be asking yourself after an error has been made is, "What will get us back on track?"

In my college years, I (David) was working as a Program Director for a camp, and responsible for 30 staff members and around 350 camp visitors each month. One day, Dean, my superior asked me to go make a deposit at the bank. "Take the camp van," he said.

I had never driven the camp van before, and it seemed kind of big and bulky. I drove into town and pulled up to the drive-through at the bank. The corner was tight. I was trying to dodge the guideposts – you know, the ones that protect the bank equipment and building so you don't get too close? Well, the posts did their job protecting the building, because as I swung around the corner, the back end of the vehicle hit one of those posts and it banged up the paneling on the side of the van.

I was terrified. I knew I did not have the money to pay for such a repair and was disappointed in myself to know I had let my boss down after he trusted me to get the job done quickly and efficiently! I had blown it!

My heart was heavy as I drove all the way back to camp. I was in fear, wondering how I would explain what I had done to a vehicle I didn't own! I pulled into the campground in such a way that Dean would not see the damage right away so that I would have the chance to explain what happened first (even though I still didn't know what I was going to say).

Dean walked out of the office and I jumped out of the van before he could get to the other side to see my very obvious transgression. I mumbled something about bumping into a post with the van as he came around the back end.

Before I could explain anything, he saw the damage . . . and burst out laughing! Now I don't mean just a giggle, but a downright belly laugh! He must have seen the shocked, remorseful look on my face and found it funny I would worry about his reaction to my blunder! "Don't worry, David, we have insurance for this kind of thing. It's no big deal. Could've happened to anybody." He continued his guffaw.

Now even with insurance, I knew there'd be a deductible, so it's not like the camp was off the hook completely. But the costs to the camp were not his priority in that moment. His priority in that moment was not to take life too seriously, and to help relieve my regret and guilt as quickly as possible. Good thing too, because it amped up my commitment to my employer big time!

I became indebted to Dean for a lifetime after that because of what he taught me regarding what was important in life. People were important. His workers were important. I was important. I spent the rest of my working days with him expressing my appreciation with dedicated and spirited service to the man who taught me the power of forgiveness.

*****

We want this to be perfectly clear in your mind:

Everyone does the best they can with what they have in each moment.

What sense does it make to condemn your employee for doing their best? That's just insane. What makes much more sense is identifying what was lacking that they missed the mark. Was it knowledge of some sort? Support? Were they distracted by another employee or by their own negative self-talk? Were they feeling ill? Was it a lapse in focus or a misjudgment based on misinformation?

While other leaders are blaming and condemning, you can be moving on to solving problems and leading your team to the next level of success.

7

Commitment Leads to Cash

"Individual commitment to a group effort - that is what makes a team work, a company work, a society work, a civilization work."

~ Vince Lombardi

Your team's commitment is crucial to your company's success. Employees who feel needed and valued by their bosses and team leaders become the most engaged workers.

Commitment is the drive that holds a company together when it's hit by the inevitable and unexpected challenges of doing business. Commitment is what makes a company survive the difficult times and come out on the other side more productive than ever. Commitment is the energy of your employees' universal devotion to insuring quality control for the various stages of planning, manufacturing, packaging, and delivery of your product or service.

Some of your employees will come with commitment in their bones – around 10% of them. It's part of their character. It comes with the package. The rest of your employees must be fostered, nurtured and shaped into dedicated heroes for your business.

Commitment is drawn out of workers when it is *inspired*. You *earn* your team members' desire and willingness to do whatever it takes for the company to grow and thrive because you've led the way by the example of your own commitment. You *show* them what commitment looks like.

Part of what heartfelt leadership means is that true commitment comes from the heart. You want your workers to buy into your dream and love it like you love it. Employees commit because they sincerely care and are personally invested. And they care and are personally invested because *you* sincerely care and are personally invested in them. They are engaged in the company's mission because *you are engaged with them.*

Know this: Workers generally do not commit to a product or a company name.

They commit to *you.*

When individuals sense sincere caring and feel appreciation for their skills and gifts, their commitment grows.

When your entire team is committed, you get to relax and trust that your employees "have your back," and are representing your company in a way that will strengthen your brand. Your profit-making machine is put on autopilot because the same drive that is in your heart is now in theirs.

So what causes an employee to be committed?

When I (Kate) think about the ideal employee, I think of my son. Alan is a personable, outgoing guy, and while growing up he was more dedicated to socializing and being a class clown than to being a great student. As an adult, he turned out to be the epitome of an employee ingrained with a strong work ethic of commitment. One of his employers, Sue

Ruane provided some vital lessons about commitment early on in his work history.

Sue was Alan's immediate supervisor when he was a camp counselor with a national youth project. Sue held high standards for performance. She did not believe it was fair to the camp kids, their parents, or the employees themselves, to let things slide. She was "tough," yet was a leader who led from her heart. She cared about the safety and overall success of the program and made sure all of the counselors knew what was expected of them and followed through on all tasks. Sue was committed to her job and taught by example.

A few years after graduation, Alan became a vintage racecar technician and racing coach. His job was to keep the owners' vintage cars in condition to race at 180 miles/hour. When his team was racing at the Watkins Glen racetrack, I got to meet some of the drivers who put their lives in Alan's hands.

What I learned from Alan's boss and the drivers he served was that my former class clown son was not only professional and competent in his expertise, he always went the extra mile (excuse the pun) to show he was committed.

Commitment is drawn out of workers when it is *inspired*.

Alan was committed to doing what was needed to get the job done. He was personally invested in the success of the individual drivers, which made him a valuable entity and face for the business. He was not only well liked, but was appreciated and *respected. His bosses were confident his reputation was a reflection of the brand they wanted.*

*****

If your team is light on commitment and heavy on apathy, our recommendation is to connect with the individual gifts and strengths you want to see more of from each employee. Let them clearly know what you expect, and notice them bringing it forth. When you see evidence of the strength displayed, make it *your commitment* to acknowledge it. Kindness makes your business more profitable.

When instilling a value of commitment in an employee, creating and holding the same standard for everyone (including yourself) is imperative. Insisting on excellence, and demonstrating it for those working for you, is crucial for your company's success.

In our experience, the greatest catalyst for commitment is a sense of ownership of the business. We're not talking about stock in the company, but a connection that goes deeper than dividends. When employees are emotionally invested in seeing a company be successful, they put their heart into their work. All workers feel a sense of purpose when they are convinced their contributions are helping the company succeed. The commitment you foster builds stronger and more effective workers, as well as leaders for your company.

In short, staff commitment leads to cash in your pocket.

8

Communication: It's Not Just Talk

"Listen and Silent are spelled with the same letters."
(Think about it.)

~ Unknown

Chances are you and your team members have been frequent victims of *sleep talking.*

You've probably heard of *sleep walking,* where people get out of bed in the middle of the night and walk around without any conscious awareness of what they are doing or saying. *Sleep talkers* move about their day and appear to be awake, but like sleep walkers, are not aware of the *unintended impact* they're having on others as they speak, nor are they able to hear fully what others are saying when it's their turn to listen.

Since sleep talkers are not fully present to what is going on in a current conversation, they are missing cues that are important in their interactions with others. Some of these cues include the look on people's faces, the feel of the energy in the room, or the content and tone of what is being spoken. [24] If they were awake, they would sense discomfort such as frustration or confusion in their partner, and then be able to appropriately respond to it. Without this awareness, the disconnect between them may deepen as both partners struggle to be heard.

The result is a conversation where one person is not effective in getting their point across, while the other struggles to remain open to the message. Ultimately, this miscommunication contributes to disengagement and inefficiency among workers. If this is going on in your workplace, it's costing you money.

When we are awake in our conversations, we have an *intended impact*. We are clear about our message and know how we want to deliver it. We craft how we say something to make it easy for the listener to take in and understand. We do not foster resistance by blaming, condemning, or making someone wrong. We are aware of how it might feel to receive our message, and adjust it accordingly to make it palatable to the listener. We want to be understood, and think about the most effective way to make that happen. We choose words that express how we feel, what we want, why something is important, and say it in a way that our listener can take it in.

At the same time, we are aware of how what we have said has "landed" on those around us. This means we are watching for our impact at the same time we are talking, awake both to what we're saying and how the other person is receiving what we've said. When we are aware of our impact, we can fine-tune what we have said or respond in a way that can help our listener comprehend our message.

When we are awake in a conversation, we know when to pause, check in with the other person, or ask a question. We sense any resistance, are able to evaluate the effectiveness of our approach as we go, and maintain a relationship connection that insures both of us are being heard.

A close friend, Ann, discovered a suspicious-appearing mole on her back, which was soon biopsied. Significant in her history was that she had been diagnosed with melanoma approximately six months prior.

When I asked how she was doing emotionally, she told me, "apparently better than some of my friends."

After going through a difficult several months with previous surgeries, waiting for pathology reports and the possibility of long-term treatment, she had already achieved a state of calm and acceptance and was not paralyzed by fear.

What she was finding, however, was that some of her friends were not listening or responding to what she was experiencing, and instead were projecting their fears onto her. They voiced their sadness, trying to say something encouraging, but were not paying attention to the impact of their words. In blurting out their fears, they missed the opportunity to be with Ann in a way that she felt heard. Unfortunately for Ann, these friends were 'asleep' and therefore did not notice their responses were unhelpful. Ann was in the presence of sleep talkers.

*****

Listening with curiosity is more helpful than reacting and spilling our personal assumptions on those we wish to help. Being an awake listener, as well as an awake talker, is crucial to remaining effective, relevant, and connected as a team in order to produce exceptional results.

One way to identify a sleep talker is to think about a conversation you have had or witnessed when voices were raised. There was likely some strong emotion present that would cause the volume to increase, maybe even to the point of yelling. When people become so frustrated that they are not being heard, they raise their voices as if in an effort to awaken their partners. When both people in a conversation raise their voices, it is likely they are both asleep.

While there is a chance that yelling at people might wake them up, there is a greater chance it will alienate them from you, making true communication and the results you desire much less likely.

When a team is affected by sleep talkers, it slows down progress, creates unintended messes, undermines trust, and creates a separateness rather than a unity within the group. All of these factors affect business productivity and income.

Awake talkers think before they speak, knowing clearly the result desired in communicating their idea. They are already aware of the possibilities of how individuals may react, and shape their message accordingly. The goal of an awake talker is not just to get something off their chest, fill time, or let off steam.

Sleep talkers are not aware of the unintended impact they're having on others as they speak.

Instead of yelling, "You piss me off!" an awake talker might say, "I feel frustrated right now because I don't think you're hearing me."

An awake talker is going somewhere with the conversation, aware of their impact, and speaks in a way that accomplishes what is intended.

An effective leader will be aware when he is falling asleep at the wheel of conversations and wake himself up. He will also be savvy enough to know how to wake up team members when they are sleep talking to recreate the connection that moves projects forward. He will know when to ask questions, ask for feedback, be open to that feedback, and be conscious of how his team is feeling about what's going on in the office. Being conversationally awake keeps team members working together, avoids costly misunderstandings, and enhances the culture that keeps your company alive and thriving.

Here are some tips for staying awake when you are speaking or listening:

Key #1: **Be Aware**

Without awareness, we will likely not respond effectively in our conversations.

Noticing how people are responding to what you have to say is vital in directing what you say next, or sometimes is an indicator of when to stop speaking. We must notice when misunderstandings are occurring, people are disengaging, or someone needs time to think about what we've said. Not being aware may also cause us to miss the opportunity to give support to someone when needed.

Awareness of your own thoughts, feelings, judgments and expectations, as well as those of others in your sphere of influence, is key to giving you guidance on how to move ahead in the conversation to get the results you want.

Key #2: **Be Curious**

Being curious means you're interested in and have a sincere desire to understand another's point of view. Frankly, people like knowing someone else is interested in them and what they have to say.

When you are curious, you do not assume you already know the answer or the solution. You don't assume you know what someone is thinking, feeling, wanting, or needing.

The natural thing to do when we're curious is to ask questions to learn more about a person, their opinion, or perspective.

It should go without saying, but we will note it anyway -- if you ask a question, listen to the answer. Respond with awareness to see where the conversation is going. Conversations are exchanges of information and perspectives, not lectures or orders about what one person wants another to do.

Key #3: **Don't Project**

It's a common trap for "unconscious" sleepy communicators to project their own fears, misinterpretations, or opinions onto someone else. When you are awake, you are tuned in to your own feelings so you will know not only what you are experiencing in the conversation, but what your partner is experiencing as well. Awake communicators don't talk just to fill the empty space. Every statement has a purpose that aligns with your intention. You know where you're going. You know what is your issue and what is theirs. You don't condemn. You support. You focus on the success of the conversation, not on controlling what they think. Sometimes reflecting what you're hearing and compassionately supporting your partner trumps sharing your own brilliant words of wisdom.

We encourage you to have fun as you practice speaking and listening while "awake." You will enjoy the increased connection with your co-workers and how it facilitates superior performance.

9

From Drama to Sanity

"Here's a trick for dealing with someone who's disappointed you:

Imagine how they looked as a very young child -- timid, a little scared, really cute, and truly not knowing any better -- and realize this is who you're dealing with now."

~ Mike Dooley

Let's face it. On the work front, there are tensions, disagreements, and arguments. It happens. Dysfunctional ways of relating are frequently the causes of our inability to resolve these differences. We resort to coercing or manipulating, withdrawing, blaming others, or giving in and doing someone else's work just to get it done. None of these ways work very effectively. Even if we get the cooperation we're after, it is often at the expense of increased personal frustration, damaged trust in the relationship, or further distancing emotionally between the parties.

In my (David's) book, *How To Stop Your Anxiety Now*, [25] I explain the concepts of the Drama Triangle and Power Sharing Triangle, and how they relate to resolving conflict. Because of its importance, we will repeat some of that discussion here. If you learn these dynamics, you will see what is going wrong in any conflict situation, and know what to do to change negative interactions or stuck places into movement and resolution.

Psychiatrist Stephen Karpman introduced the concept of the Drama Triangle, [26] also called the Victim Triangle, as a way of helping us understand the roles we play while interacting with others - roles that lead to miscommunication, dysfunction, lack of cooperation, and a downward push in productivity and production.

Karpman explained that whenever there is conflict in a relationship, we could look to identify one of three roles we are playing in that relationship that is contributing to the problem. In doing so, we can begin to see more clearly how we are creating our own ill feelings and sabotaging our success. Look for how these patterns may be occurring in your workplace.

Victim Role

The first role identified in the Drama Triangle is that of Victim. The Victim role is distinguished from a real victim by writing it with a capital "V."

We are real victims if our house is broken into, and through no fault of our own someone has caused hurt by damaging or taking our property. We are also victims if we are targets of drive-by shootings, of a sexual assault, or have our investments stolen by an unscrupulous investor or broker.

However, often we participate in being victimized in relationships. In these instances, we are Victims with a capital "V" because we are giving up our power to protect ourselves and are participating in maintaining our own dilemma. We may feel ganged up on, criticized, blamed, smothered, or controlled by another. Like the genuine victim, we often feel helpless, powerless, and hopeless when playing this role. In this case, however, our victimization is only an illusion.

Drama Triangle

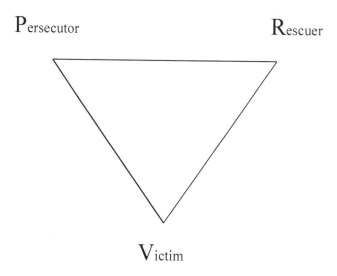

Persecutor   Rescuer

Victim

Although we may be a real victim when our house is robbed, we become a Victim on the Triangle if we are robbed several times because we keep forgetting to lock our door. When we are in partnership with our assailant, we are no longer a "victim," but a "Victim."

The same is true in workplace environments. Although we at times feel like victims of circumstance, employee problems, misunderstandings, or unambitious workers, we are not victims, and pretending we are keeps us from the success we seek.

We play Victim when we do not acknowledge our part in creating our misunderstandings, choose not to reach out for help, or wait for someone else to solve our business challenge. Difficult as it may be, this responsibility lies solely on each of us.

Rescuer Role

The second position on the Drama Triangle is that of Rescuer. The "R" in the upper right hand corner of the Triangle refers to this role.

As Rescuers, we have common co-dependent traits like over-caring, doing more than our share, or assuming what people need. Rescuers tend to be nice people who really want to help others, but are slow in seeing that what looks like helping to them may not be helping at all. This corner on the Triangle is often labeled with the phrase "trying to help." A Rescuer puts out a lot of energy to assist others, but frequently feels betrayed, especially when his or her efforts are refused or unappreciated. They may not stop to think what they are offering may not be what their co-worker is wanting or needing, and so offer the wrong things. This results in the efforts of "trying to help" without really helping.

Samples of Rescuing behaviors include: doing more than our share of the work (ideas, talking, etc.), assuming what someone wants or needs rather than asking directly, over-supporting, and caretaking. This can leave us feeling anxious and out of control, angry, unappreciated, disappointed, and confused about what to do next.

Real victims (of a burning house) hope, long for, and need

real rescuers (firefighters). Those playing a Victim Role, though hoping for a Rescuer, really need someone who is not just trying to help. They need someone who really helps by getting off the Drama Triangle and choosing a more powerful way of interacting.

Persecutor Role

The third position on the Drama Triangle is that of Persecutor, labeled with a capital "P." Persecutors are critical, condemning, rigid or controlling. They may come across demanding,   self-centered,   and   overtly manipulative. Sometimes Persecutors are passive-aggressive and you feel tricked. You can often tell when you are in the presence of a Persecutor because you don't feel respected or free to make your own decisions or choices. Although many Persecutors are forceful, loud, and overbearing, some are subtle, and control with their tone of voice and choice of words more than their volume. Some use guilt as subtler form of persecuting.

Other examples of persecuting behaviors include yelling, swearing, intimidating, threatening, ordering around, ignoring, sneering, expressions of disgust, angry sighs, or manipulative questions. The attempt behind these actions is to get the other person to conform to what the Persecutor wants without leaving freedom of choice. This stance can be characterized with the phrase "trying to blame," reflecting its critical and controlling tone.

You may indeed need a worker to conform to a company policy or request. We are about to suggest powerful ways to do this without manipulating or coercing.

You can imagine that living or working with a Persecutor can leave one feeling very anxious, off balance, straining to keep one's self esteem, and drained of energy. It is difficult to perform at one's best in the presence of a Persecutor.

The roles and their accompanying behaviors are summarized in the chart on the next page.

Drama Triangle Summary

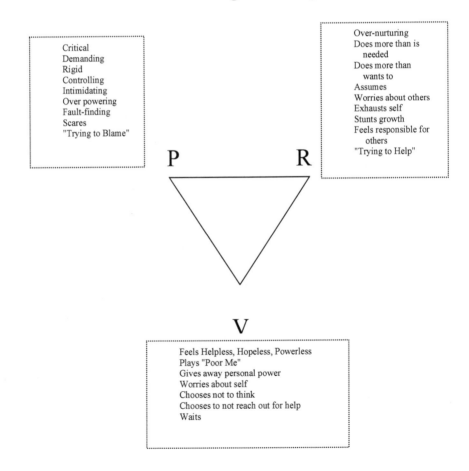

Critical
Demanding
Rigid
Controlling
Intimidating
Over powering
Fault-finding
Scares
"Trying to Blame"

Over-nurturing
Does more than is needed
Does more than wants to
Assumes
Worries about others
Exhausts self
Stunts growth
Feels responsible for others
"Trying to Help"

P   R

V

Feels Helpless, Hopeless, Powerless
Plays "Poor Me"
Gives away personal power
Worries about self
Chooses not to think
Chooses to not reach out for help
Waits

Whenever we adopt any of the behaviors, attitudes and feelings of the Drama Triangle roles, we are likely to feel uncomfortable at best, or miserable and hopeless at worst. More importantly, we're going to have trouble getting things done without an excessive amount of effort. You cannot afford this wasted energy.

Playing any of the three roles can leave us feeling anxious and preoccupied, unable to bring our own best to the job. Victims have trouble finding their most powerful selves to contribute fully. Rescuers feel exhausted, wondering how to motivate their employees who do not seem to be responding. Persecutors feel agitated because they are frequently upset, having to use large amounts of energy to get the outcomes they seek. They may be unsure how to guarantee the results they need in the future without being demanding.

You can see that being able to determine which role(s) you and your staff are playing can help identify how you may be participating in creating your own discomfort. Know that playing these roles is common. Most of us engage in these interactions on a regular basis, and are unconscious of the dynamics.

If you understand what's being said here, you are noticing how you defeat yourself, and ultimately, how you will free yourself. You are also noticing, no doubt, how some of your workers defeat themselves, and what they may need to change to serve your company with their fullest potential.

The question is, once we discover what roles we are playing, what do we do differently besides playing Victim, Rescuer, or Persecutor? That's what the Power Sharing Triangle is all about. Read on.

10

How To Share Power For Maximum Performance

"If life isn't about human beings and living in harmony, then I don't know what it's about."

~ Orlando Bloom

Now that you know how to diagnose drama in your workplace, you need tools for shifting the dynamics to interactions that will be more productive and profitable. Three of those powerful ways are summed up in the concept of the Power Sharing Triangle. [27]

The Power Sharing Triangle shows at a glance what we could do differently once we discovered we were caught in the unsatisfying roles of Victim, Rescuer, or Persecutor.

Legitimate Need Response

When I play the Victim, I am acting helpless. I may feel emotionally assaulted or trapped. I have trouble seeing a way out. I may have trouble knowing what I need in the moment. The first step out of my predicament is to identify what I need.

Power Sharing Triangle

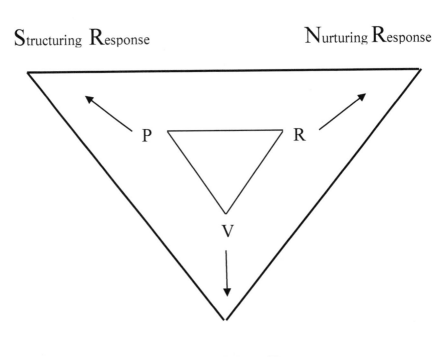

Structuring Response

Nurturing Response

Legitimate Need Response

Some ways to identify needs include paying attention to body signals - like muscle tension, to intuition - like the desire to speak up, or to ask myself the question directly, "What do I need?"

When we do this, we are stepping back off the Victim corner of the Drama Triangle to a corner named Legitimate

Need Response (LNR). Here we are discovering what our legitimate need is and taking some action to get that need met.

When I step back to the LNR corner, I can get the big picture view of what I have been doing to myself. I may discover needs such as:

- I need to call an associate for support.

- I need to ask for help from my supervisor.

- I need to think of a solution and share it.

- I need to collaborate with a worker to get to a solution.

- I need some quiet to think this through.

- I need to remind someone of his or her responsibility.

- I need to instill a consequence.

- I need to let go of my resentment.

- I need to stand up for me.

Once the need is identified, I either take action to meet that need or ask for help from someone.

Speaking from our LNR might look like this:

"I'm irritated right now. I need you to give this matter attention immediately. Will you?"

"I'll save us both some time . . . I can't discuss this at the moment. Will you call me back at 1 o'clock?"

"I want to see that report before you leave tonight. Do you need anything more from me to get it finished?"

"I'm aware that there's some tension between you and Judy. I need that to stop. How can I help you resolve it?"

These actions result in me refusing to remain a Victim as a leader or co-worker, and I actually start solving my problem. I redistribute power in the system by doing what gets us unstuck, instead of waiting for others to "get it," or feeling I'm powerless to change the situation.

Nurturing Response

If my tendency is to Rescue, I have another place I can save myself some misery and move off the Drama Triangle. I can step back to a place called Nurturing Response (NR). The name of this corner implies that I do not give up my intention or interest in supporting, but offer my assistance in a more powerful way. I continue to extend my energy in a way that is genuinely helpful, not just "trying to help."

When we step back off the Rescuer corner, we can actually feel the difference in our bodies. In our workshops, we will often place these diagrams on the floor with tape and have people walk through how it feels to speak from these different perspectives. In general, the Rescuer place feels burdensome, like a lot of work. There is kind of a fragile hope from this place with little confidence that my intervention will actually do much.

From Nurturing Response, I feel empowered again, because

I am now sharing the power with my former Victim, giving up responsibility that is not mine and calling this individual forth to act on his or her own behalf. This is genuine helping.

A Nurturing Response is usually warm and caring, with belief in the other that he can solve his problem. I do not solve it for him, though I may offer to help. I let the person know I trust in their ability and choice to get out of their dilemma with me supporting fully, but not being enmeshed. I am truly caring, focused and sincere, but from a distance that now allows freedom for my co-worker to claim their personal power and move ahead.

Nurturing Responses might look like this:

"That must feel awful. I'm sorry that happened to you. What can I do to help?"

"I know you can do it! You've overcome situations like this before!"

"You are a bright and creative individual. I trust in your ability to solve this problem."

"I can see you are very discouraged about this. Do you think you can hang in there until the project is finished?"

"What do you think you can do about it?"

"What would you like from me that would help you?"

"I believe in you."

Remember, as a Nurturing Responder, we don't assume we know what a person needs. We also don't steal someone's personal power by doing more than our share. We think and choose carefully, committing only to those things we are really committed to doing.

Structuring Response

The final position on the Power Sharing Triangle is the Structuring Response. You can see by the name that this position retains some of the quality of directing or guiding in a respectful (and genuinely helpful) way.

The Structuring Response gives choices, shows how, makes requests, or sets boundaries while believing in the power of the other to act on his or her own behalf. In contrast to the Persecutor corner, there is an absence of condemnation or judgment, though feelings may still be expressed. There is often strong support provided from this place.

Examples of Structuring Responses:

"Stop that. I mean it!"

"It's not possible for me to loosen up the funds for a raise right now, but I will see what I can do to let you know we appreciate your contributions to the company."

Your drinking is affecting your performance at work. If you continue this behavior, it's going to put your job at risk."

"This is how I want you to submit the brief." (shows how)

"We all show up on time. It's part of the respect we offer each other here."

POWER SHARING TRIANGLE SUMMARY

Gives Direction
Supplies Information
Shows How
Sets Limits
Guides
Provides Options
Makes Requests
Believes in Other
States What's
    Important
Provides Safety

Supports
Encourages
Understands
Invites to Think
Believes in Other
Gives Reassurance
Doesn't Fix
Shows Concern
Acknowledges Real
    Need
Responds to
    Feelings

Structuring **R**esponse   **N**urturing **R**esponse

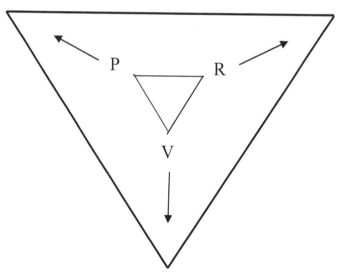

Legitimate **N**eed **R**esponse

Accepts Personal Power
Identifies Need
Takes Action
Asks for Help

85

For us as Structuring Responders, there is a solid foundation in our belief system that we trust the problem can be solved, and are inviting others to step up to the plate and do their share. There is a sense of real clarity and an absence of negative controlling, coercion, and blaming. We no longer feel like we have to force someone to do something. We take the pressure off ourselves by letting the other person be more powerful in the relationship.

Stepping off any of the Drama Triangle corners can serve to lower our anxiety levels, reduce worry, empower our responses, and let us relax and enjoy our relationships more. We don't have to feel helpless, manipulate others to get our way, or over-nurture to the point of exhaustion. What bosses tend to like most about this model is that it reduces stress, empowers and engages employees in a compelling way, and work gets done faster.

Here are some ways to practice these techniques:

A)   This week, watch a Fox News program or listen to Rush Limbaugh or a politician explain his or her position and look for where the characters are playing Victim, Rescuer, or Persecutor roles. Some people use these principles consciously and depend on the drama of the Triangle to keep viewers/listeners interested in their show. You may notice it works quite effectively! Use this as a way to practice noticing how people play the roles, and how it deepens conflict and polarizes people, pushing a solution farther away.

B)   Observe yourself and relationships around you to become aware of how you and others slip into the Drama Triangle roles. Do not condemn yourself or others with what you notice. Instead, be amused and pleased that you are becoming more aware.

C)   Identify specific behaviors that represent how you play the Drama Triangle corners. Consciously design alternatives that represent more helpful responses from the Power Sharing Triangle.

*****

Example 1:

Behavior: I repeatedly step in to do Mary's job for her since she (a victim) complains of getting stressed with the fast pace.

My Drama Corner: Rescuer

Alternative Response: "Mary, I see you are running behind with getting your job done; what is it you need to do so you can catch up?"

My Power Sharing Corner: Nurturing Response

Example 2:

Behavior: I gathered my team together in the morning and with a pointed finger and warned them that they better make the sales quota today, since they cost the company $10,000 the day before.

My Drama Corner: Persecutor

Alternative Response: "Okay team, yesterday our performance was off our usual excellent mark. We have a big day ahead of us today . . . let's work together to stay focused and beat our quota. Ask for help if you need it, and let's message victories throughout the day. I want to hear from each of you twice today - before lunch and also by mid-afternoon."

My Power Sharing Corner: Structuring Response

Fill in these blanks with examples from your workplace:

Behavior 1:

My Drama Corner:

Alternative Response:

My Power Sharing Corner:

Behavior 2:

My Drama Corner:

Alternative Response:

My Power Sharing Corner:

Behavior 3:

My Drama Corner:

Alternative Response:

My Power Sharing Corner:

11

The Alliance: A Successful Team's Secret Weapon

" Great leadership is not for the weak of heart . . . It is for those with the biggest hearts. "

~ Kate Sholonski

Formulating Your Team Culture

You have a tool and a process to create the team culture you desire. No more waiting around and hoping things get better. With an Alliance, you know *how* to make it better.

An Alliance is a set of agreements that strengthens relationships and builds stronger, more effective and cooperative teams.

Most organizations have job descriptions and mission statements about what is expected of workers in terms of tasks or performance output. The Alliance we are describing is a similar understanding about how individuals in a workgroup will treat and support each other to increase their performance measures. It's a design and commitment to the treaties that govern social interactions and relationships on the job.

There is no manipulation, power play, coercing, or frustration in trying to get people to do what you want them to do, because there is buy-in by everyone participating. No one is on the outside. No one is seen or treated as less important than anyone else. It is an equal partnership that works because both you and your staff know exactly what they need to in order to bring out their best performance, and you have agreed together to make it happen.

Alliances are created within an atmosphere of respect, honest disclosure, understanding, communication of needs and wants, and a commitment to desired behaviors.

Through the process of the Alliance creation, ideas and requests are discussed until everyone agrees to invest their energy in support of the common relationship goals. The end result is a universal connection among employees, yielding a cooperative synergy in the team.

Here is a method of Alliance creation we have found very powerful in our work with teams. Can you pull out a few pointers from the following to help create the team you want and need?

Step 1: Create the foundation for your workplace culture.

You don't build a house without a strong foundation, and you don't build a business successfully without one, either. It is important that your team agrees on what elements are key for optimum cooperation and productivity. As you establish your culture's foundation, you may consider incorporating qualities such as openness, respect, honesty, and non-judgmental communication as cornerstones. For Zig Ziglar, the foundation looked like this:

"The foundation stones for balanced success are honesty, character, integrity, faith, love and loyalty."

Start by identifying your foundational Alliance elements.

1) Ask your team to **think** about what would make them look forward to coming to work every day. What characteristics of the ideal work environment would they like to experience as being part of your team?

2) Have the group **brainstorm and discuss** these characteristics you all want as a team that will contribute to the highest production of the group.

3) Have someone volunteer to scribe or **capture** all notes on a white board or flip chart and then type and email the notes to everyone.

Examples:
- Be treated with respect
- Speak to each other without raised voices
- Have fun
- Be acknowledged for our contributions
- Receive frequent feedback from coworkers or boss
- Have direct, honest communication
- Eliminate put-downs

Step 2: Define what those desires *mean* to each team member.

Since concepts like "respect" or "support" can have a different meaning to each person, these perspectives must be shared in order for each team member to understand what the others are thinking. This yields clarity about what workers specifically want, as well as clues for how team members can respond. It also gives insight into what kinds of behaviors become roadblocks or irritations that get in the way of their coworkers performing at the top of their game.

Example: "Be treated with respect" might mean:

- To be spoken to calmly – normal tone of voice
- To be asked to do something rather than be ordered
- To share opinions briefly without lectures
- If I make a mistake, tell me privately
- We will not talk behind each others' backs

A nice team-building bonus is when someone offers an example of what they would like to see, and then finds out others often want the same thing.

Step 3: Committing to the Agreements.

Once the key elements are established of what team members want, and all speak specifically to what that means to them, agreements need to be made regarding making these changes real.

To clarify what an agreement is, let us first begin by addressing what it is NOT.

An agreement is NOT:

- Something decided upon without discussion
- Something only the boss wants
- Something stated and agreed to without documenting
- Something that is for show or merely a formality
- An opportunity to force personal desires down other team members' throats

An Agreement IS:

- Something that is co-created and mutually agreed to through sufficient discussion that all concerned clearly understand

- Documented so everyone can refer to it in the future

- A promise from each employee to honor their co-workers' requests to the best of their ability

- A design that will allow for, address and correct any errors or misses as it is practiced

- Always open for fine-tuning and changes, agreed upon by all involved as time goes on

Example: "Do we all agree to honor the suggestion to speak respectfully to one another?" Each team member must indicate yay or nay. Agreement must be obtained from all participants for it to become part of the Alliance.

Repeat this process for each element of the Alliance.

If you cannot get full agreement on the items, go deeper or rephrase the requests until agreement can be made.

Making the commitment means everyone on the team now agrees to honor the requests so that each team member feels supported by common agreements.

When the commitments are made, there is an invisible and motivational bond created that makes the Alliance more than the sum of the parts. This is the magic of synergy.

In any of these steps, emotions may surface and are to be welcomed. No one should be judged for how they feel.

Step 4: Making it Real: Establishing Accountability

After completing all of the steps above, the final step is to make it real by actually honoring all the agreements. There is a difference between understanding what co-workers need and actually delivering it. In this stage, we expand beyond agreement and commitment to accountability.

There is a powerful engagement in the process of the team building as each member commits to being accountable to the agreements, since it automatically creates equal responsibility for a successful Alliance.

***

**Think
Discuss
Capture
Define
Agree
Commit**

***

We have often observed that this step excites and energizes individuals, almost as if each is being heard for the first time. At other times we notice this may cause some fear or resistance, which needs to be noted and dealt with in order to avoid subsequent sabotage of the Alliance.

More hints to insure a successful Alliance:

- Be sure to schedule the alliance meetings at a time you will not be interrupted and when everyone can be present.

- Do not rush through the process. People will need time to think, feel and commit to ideas discussed. If necessary, break up the Alliance into separate meetings making sure not to let more than a few days pass in between. Always review what had been agreed upon up to that point.

- Have someone volunteer to scribe or capture all notes on a white board or flip chart and then type and email the notes to everyone.

- Every element of the Alliance must have 100% agreement. This does not mean every employee wants the same thing. What it does mean is that every person speaks openly about what they need, and then each team member agrees to find a way those requests can be honored without compromising his own personal needs.

  Example: Kate needs to have fun, and David needs periods when he will not be interrupted or distracted. All team members (including David) agree not to interfere with Kate creating fun for herself, and all team members (including Kate) respect David's need for personal focus.

- Avoid blaming or finger pointing if anyone misses honoring an agreement. In fact, discuss ahead how you will handle situations if/when the Alliance is overlooked.

- Find a mutually agreeable way that you can help one another get back on track, such as a hand signal or a code word. Be sure to include this in the Alliance notes.

    Example: One team agreed on using the code word "radishes" to call attention to the need to shift a discussion and avoid triggering reactions or repeating old, unhelpful patterns.

- Schedule regular "Culture Check" meetings to celebrate successful implementation of the Alliance. This time may also be used to reflect on the missteps and how they can be avoided in the future.

- Forgive yourself and everyone else for the missteps. Commitment does not mean perfection. Room must be allowed for slip-ups, but they should be acknowledged without blame or criticism, with a renewed intention to do better the next time.

- Have fun with this! Alliances help build healthy relationships and the process of co-creating, practicing and honoring the agreements is more likely to be successful when the process is enjoyable.

Building an Alliance is a process of more depth than having people simply writes requests down on paper or emailing suggestions. It requires discussion, listening, planning, commitment, compromise, and a conscious investment of energy, all for the sake of assisting everyone in fulfilling the company's mission. Going through the process of creating an Alliance is, in itself, a relationship strengthening experience.

The reason why alliances are so effective is because it shares the power of creating success.

Keep communication open as you have ongoing discussions, expansion of ideas, and celebrations of your successes. It is well worth the effort! When your employees are not busy creating drama, they will be able to focus more energy on generating a faster track to your prosperity.

12

From Wealthy to *Really* Wealthy

"There is more to life than just increasing its speed."
~ Mahatma Gandhi

A handsome young gentleman walked into my counseling office one day. I could tell he was a hard worker, outwardly confident, with a body built like he came from the Schwarzenegger family. He had pulled up to my office in a stylish up-scale SUV, and was anxious to sit down in my office and start talking.

Before his butt actually hit the chair, he began his speech. "I wanted to be a millionaire by the time I was 40. I beat my goal by one year. I'm 39 and just crossed the million dollar mark..." After about a 10-minute orientation to his dream-come-true financial life, I paused him for a moment.

"I'm happy for your success, yet I don't quite understand something. If things are going so well for you, why are you here?"

His mood darkened, eyes dropping toward the floor. His speech slowed. In a quieter voice, he said, "My wife is leaving me. I have spent my life working my tail off to reach my goal, and now I'm losing my family. In fact, she's gone, and so are my kids. I want to know if you can help me get my family back."

His formerly confident broad shoulders drooped a bit, and the innocent and wounded "little boy" showed through like a whipped pup. My heart softened for him, too, and we shared together the grief of his losses, of his life falling apart...

*****

Making money is fun, but it's not as fun as what money can buy. And it's not as fun as what money can't buy. My client wanted something his money couldn't buy him. And so do we all. We are all seeking joy, peace, relationships that work, to feel good about ourselves – happiness.

If you ever took a psychology class in high school or college, you may have learned that money is a "secondary reinforcer." That means that it has no value in and of itself. It is only valuable for what you can do with it.

The principles we teach definitely make businesses more money. We've shared many of these principles in this book. We want you to make more of it than you've ever made before. And what's more, it's important to us that you ENJOY making your money.

As you know, every day, every hour, every moment that goes by, is one we never get back. If we let it go by without enjoying it, we have a 100% failure rate of how we used that time, and the chance of changing that is 0%. Wouldn't it be a shame if you got to the end of your life and all you had to show for it was a bunch of accomplishments? If you've missed the joy, you've missed why you came here. If you are not at peace, what good does your stock fund balance have, even if it is growing?

The material things themselves cannot generate life satisfaction. In fact, research shows that only about 10% of our happiness is due to external factors. [28]

Nobel prize-winning psychologist Daniel Kahneman, together with economist Angus Deaton, published a hallmark study which found that in the United States, happiness levels off at incomes of around $75,000 a year. [29]   After we have our basic needs met, there is little correlation between money and the ability to enjoy life.

Do you know how long the thrill of getting a new house lasts? Research indicates about six months on average. Do you know how long the joy of getting that new job you always wanted will stay with you? About six months. How long do lottery winners hang onto their happiness after winning the lottery? About six months. [30]

From new car owners to hot-fudge sundae eaters, from newlyweds to lotto winners, external factors, even if exhilarating at first, cannot sustain a sense of joy. Joy comes from within. And most of us need to be taught how to sustain that joy.

The following story illustrates all too well how confused we can get regarding how to invest our time for life's greatest satisfactions.

The American Investment Banker

An ambitious American investment banker was at the pier of a small coastal Mexican village when a small boat with just one fisherman docked. Inside the small boat were several large yellow fin tuna. The American complimented the Mexican on the quality of his fish and asked how long it took to catch them. The Mexican replied that it was only a little while.

The American then asked why didn't he stay out longer and catch more fish? The Mexican said he had enough to support his family's immediate needs. The American then asked, "But what do you do with the rest of your time?" The Mexican fisherman said, "I sleep late, fish a little, play with my children, take siesta with my wife, Maria, and stroll into the village each evening, where I sip wine and play guitar with my amigos. I have a full and busy life."

The American scoffed, "I could help you. You should spend more time fishing, and with the proceeds buy a bigger boat. With the proceeds from the bigger boat, you could buy several boats. In time, you would have a fleet of fishing boats. Instead of selling your catch to a middleman, you would sell directly to the processor, eventually opening your own cannery. You would control the product, processing and distribution. You would move to Mexico City, then LA and eventually NYC where you could run your expanding enterprise."

The Mexican fisherman asked, "But, how long will this all take?"

"You could accomplish it in 15-20 years" said the American.

"But what then?"

The American laughed and said that's the best part. "When the time is right you would announce an IPO and sell your company stock to the public and become very rich, you would make millions."

"Millions . . . Then what?"

The American said, "Then you would retire. Move to a small coastal fishing village where you would sleep late, fish a little, play with your kids, take siesta with your wife, and stroll to the village in the evenings, where you could sip wine and play your guitar with your amigos." [31]

*****

Yes, making money is important, but your happiness is more important.

Do you know what brings you happiness? How often do you step over it in the present because you are so focused on the future that you miss the gifts of today? Don't let other people shape your perception of what joy is for you. Or what success is.

When it comes down to being all alone, with no one around to impress . . . when the quiet settles in as you sit down with a beer or glass of wine with nothing to prove to anyone, how do you feel about yourself . . . about who you are? How connected do you feel to your purpose in life, why you came here to the planet, and what you're learning about humanity and spirituality while you're here?

Regardless of your answers to the questions above, we have some suggestions about how to take the next steps, how to make yourself feel alive, how to make your heart sing.

Start by carving out some quiet time – a half hour or more, and jot down your responses to the following questions:

- What makes you happy?

- How often are you enjoying the things, people, or experiences that make you happy?

- What keeps you from enjoying the things that make you happy?

- What would need to change in order for you to allow happiness to be a more constant companion?

- What did you hope to accomplish in creating your business?

- Besides making money, what is it that keeps you working hard?

- What stories are you telling yourself about not making yourself a priority? What beliefs do you hold that limit your ability to feel joy and peace?

- What personal needs are not being fully addressed in your lifestyle?

- How can you give those needs a higher priority? What help do you need to accomplish this?

- When you reach the end of your life, what memories will you be most grateful for?

*****

Please don't skip these questions. If you don't have time now, give yourself the gift of scheduling it in your calendar to explore them later.

Congratulations! You are well on your way to creating the wonderful life you deserve! You are on your way from financial wealth to complete wealth!

13

A Special Message for the Boss

The Heartfelt Connection with Yourself

"Finding your inner peace, one has to achieve the ability to live in harmony with oneself and the world."

~ Julandie Scholtz

While you meet the day-to-day challenges and struggles necessary to keep your business alive and thriving, we want to make sure you don't lose track of your Self. Chances are you had hopes to make a difference . . . to create something that will influence other peoples' lives in a positive way. You probably also dreamed of financial freedom and to have control over your choices in life, yet somehow along the way of building your business, you may have forgotten to nurture the most important part of that business – YOU.

We all read and hear a lot about the importance of self-care in regards to our diet, exercise and stress management. These are all important in maintaining a healthy life, yet there is a deeper need within that is calling for your attention. That deep need is to remember your value and worth, and we're not talking about your bank account! We're talking about having a life abundant with peace, joy, and meaning.

To be a leader and facilitator of positive change, it is important the process begins with you. When your head is on straight and aligned with your heart, your life vision will remain clear. You will stay focused on the WHY you are in the business you're in. You will be a better boss to your employees and a better partner in all your relationships.

We encourage you to maintain a healthy relationship with yourself and assess regularly how you're managing your daily challenges. We urge you to be honest with yourself and what you need so you can get through your day without feeling drained and strained. When you keep your priorities clear of the erroneous belief that you must suffer in order for your business to grow, your journey to success will mean as much to you as arriving at the very success you seek!

Here are some habits that will help you maintain the connection with your Self that serves as the foundation for your connection with others:

Practicing Presence. Being present is about keeping your attention in the 'Now'. Be aware of your thoughts, your words and your actions. Do they make you feel better, or are they causing you suffering? As you practice being aware, you will eventually notice you are always making choices. When you notice your choices are causing some ill feelings within yourself, look again. Decide if this is going to create the kind of life you long to live, one of peace and joy, or if it will keep you stalled, experiencing lack, or leave you emotionally drained. Awareness is your first step to change, so being present with yourself is a key to knowing what to do next.

Meditation. Taking even a few minutes a day to be quiet and allow your thoughts to slow down or even stop will help you experience the power of *stillness*. Your greatest guidance comes from within, but it is difficult to hear that advice in the busyness of everyday activities. There is magic in stillness. There is wisdom in stillness. There is clarity in stillness. There is peace in stillness.

If you have never experienced meditation before, don't knock it 'til you've tried it! You may be one who resists meditation, seeing it as a waste of time. Think of it this way: Are you at your best when you are relaxed and centered, or when you're stressed and anxious? Give meditation a chance to calm and shift you to a place of greater serenity and ease. After meditating, people often find themselves re-energized and focused, increasing productive activities. [32]

The benefits of meditation increase with practice. If it stimulates some agitation for you at first, notice what thoughts it brings up. If you have a belief that you must be doing something to be valuable, ask yourself how much must be accomplished before you can rest or give yourself a break? If you do indeed feel more peaceful, enjoy it. You deserve it. Allow it to help you meet the challenges of your business and life in a more powerful way.

Sit down in a comfortable and quiet place, close your eyes, and focus on your breathing. Focusing on your breathing immediately brings you into the present moment where worrying or regretting is more difficult. Breathe slowly in and out, allowing your body to relax with each exhalation. With each exhaling breath, let go of any thoughts or concerns that are bothering you, and keep your attention on your breathing. After a few minutes, open your eyes and notice the positive impact this quiet time has had on how you feel and your readiness to go back to work refreshed.

One woman reported:

"The greatest thing for me is experiencing the peace and lack of fear. Because I feel less fear, I have greater confidence and trust that whatever is on my plate will work out. When my mind is not wrapped up in worries of what could go wrong, I am able to enjoy the peace in the present moment. Since meditation has become part of my daily practice, I am freed up to experience greater creativity and productivity in my work and private life."

Rampage of Appreciation. Here's an exercise that's fun and feels good too! We learned it from Esther and Jerry Hicks. [33] It will put you in a psychological and spiritual space that brings the best out of you and maximizes your creativity and energy.

Begin by looking around your immediate environment and gently noticing something that pleases you. Try to hold your attention on this pleasing object as you consider how wonderful, beautiful, or useful it is. And as you focus upon it longer, your positive feeling about it will increase.

Now notice your improved feeling, and be appreciative of the way you feel. Then, once your good feeling is noticeably stronger than when you began, look around your environment and choose another pleasing object for your positive attention.

Make it your objective to choose objects or situations that easily evoke your appreciation, rather than finding things that trouble you, creating a desire to fix them.

For example, while standing in the line at the grocery store, you may think:

- It's great that they keep this place so clean.

- I like how friendly that check-out person is.

- I appreciate the way that mother is interacting with her child.

- That's a good-looking jacket on that woman.

- I love the sun shining in the window like that.

- I'm glad to have the money to buy this food.

- That scanning equipment is a real asset to save time.

- I appreciate all the sales I found today.

- I'm grateful I am physically able to carry these groceries.

Once you have made a decision that nothing is more important than feeling good, and you have decided that you are going to consciously look for something to appreciate, the object of your attention has now become the feeling of appreciation. The snowball effect of this exercise will keep elevating you to your most productive frame of mind, and it trains your mind to see possibilities you didn't see before.

Start by taking a few minutes to do this every day. Then do it several times a day, more and more frequently, until it becomes a habit. Then you will be consistently creating your own good feelings automatically and effortlessly, and you will bring your best self to your family, community, and work!

Next Best Feeling Thought. Self-Care demands that you stay in charge of your thoughts and train them in the direction that gives you the results you want. Next Best Feeling Thought [34] is an exercise that systematically points you in a positive direction, no matter how deep you find yourself in a hole.

Let's say you notice a thought going through your mind, "I'll never get this finished in time!" It's sometimes difficult to jump from that thought to, "I'm going to handle this one with ease," but it may come to pass if you focus on whatever *next best feeling* thought you can find.

It's like taking the next step up a mountain. One step at a time – one thought at a time – you move yourself toward what you want, refusing to stay stuck in discouragement.

So the next best feeling thought after "I'll never get this finished in time," might become "Taking a break always helps me think more clearly." Gradually, you keep pursuing the next best feeling thought until you raise your awareness and energy to a point of moving forward. It might go like this:

"I'll never get this finished in time." →

"Taking a break always helps me think more clearly." →

"Breathe deep, and let the fear go." →

"I might be able to finish in time if I ask for help." →

"I'll break this down into smaller steps and ask Jim and Susan to be responsible for some of them." →

"I've always made it before. I'll make it again." →

"I think I can actually see the light at the end of the tunnel on this thing." →

"If I put my mind to it, I can do anything." →

"I'm going to handle this one with ease."

You've climbed the mountain one step at a time, and you made it! This is a great exercise to get you out of overwhelm, generate new ideas to break through a stuck place, and generate hope and optimism out of a dark and desperate beginning.

As you move ahead from here, we urge you to keep in mind you are the foundation of your business' success, and it simply makes sense for you to take care of yourself in every way. Be generous, yet know what doesn't serve you and say "no" to anything that will interfere with your highest good.

The litmus test for assessing how you're doing is simple. Check in with how you feel. If you feel stressed, overwhelmed, scared and feel like you have to keep on running to catch up, stop and reassess what you're doing. If you notice you feel more peace and joy, and have more focused energy for your work, congratulate yourself and continue to practice what feels good. You are never done, so stay tuned in. . . .to yourself, that is. Your heart will always tell you what you need.

Appendix

Meditation for Busy People

In my practice as a psychologist, I have been asked that if I could distill all of my psychological strategies down to the best of the best, the silver bullet, the crème de la crème, the mother of all healing techniques, the one thing people could do to maintain health, open up channels to success, reduce stress, defeat depression and anxiety, and step into lasting joy, what would that be? In other words, is there a best advice I could give in 5 seconds that would help just about anyone with just about anything?

The answer is yes.

Actually, I can do it less than five seconds. I can do it in less than one second. If there is one thing you can do to lower blood pressure and decrease stress, let go of grief, get clarity of mind, unleash your potential within, shift you out of your stuck places of self-defeating thoughts and feelings, and keep yourself in the winner's circle, it is this: meditation.

Meditation has two foundational ingredients: conscious breathing, and releasing thoughts. Although there are many advantages to establishing a regular meditation practice that takes you out of the world and into yourself for periods of time (we highly recommend this), Kate and I would like to share several techniques for how you can get the benefit of meditation with brief interventions, or while you are doing something else. It's meditation for busy people!

There are several types of active breathing that we can recommend, depending on what you'd like to accomplish.

(1) The first method is called **Alternate Nostril Breathing**. Here's how it works:

Gently rest your right thumb against your right nostril and take a breath in and out. Then release your thumb and place your forefinger gently against your left nostril and take one breath. Repeat this pattern 27 times, 3 times a day.

This type of breathing has been shown to lower blood pressure and engage your parasympathetic nervous system in a way that calms both your body and your mind. It's a way to wind down, let go, take a break, and release stress. It rebalances your energy and that racing thinker of yours. The practice automatically invites your body to relax, and your mind to release its stress-inducing multi-tasking. [35]

(2) A second type of breathing we'd like to share is called **Bellows Breath.** Place your hand on your belly and pretend your stomach is actually your lungs. Breathe deeply and rapidly in and out of your gut through your nose, allowing your hand to be pushed out by your belly. What we're going for here is three in-and-out breaths per second. You'll notice a lot of action in your diaphragm. You can feel the sides and back of your torso expand with each inhaling as well. Your entire lower torso becomes a "bellows" as you breathe deep into your stomach and pelvis to clear tension being held in your gut. You'll also feel action at the back of your neck and in your chest (as you chest supports your diaphragm's movement). This

exercise is a bit vigorous. Start at about 15 seconds and gradually add time as you become more experienced.

This type of breathing can be very energizing and is a good substitute of taking a brisk walk when doing so is not possible, or as a substitute for grabbing that next cup of coffee.

(3) A third breathing technique is called the **Ocean Breath**. It is good for inducing sleep, one of the essential habits needed by successful business people. You must get good rest to be at your best. Sleep is not only necessary for your body to stay healthy, but restores your energy tank that allows you to keep going day after day at your important tasks. We often think we get more done if we push ourselves beyond our normal sleep patterns, but this is mostly an illusion that it creates better performance.

To get the hang of this one, go stand in front of a mirror and breathe in such a way as to fog up the mirror. If you don't have a mirror handy, hold your hand a few inches in front of your mouth and breathe into it as you would when fogging up a mirror.

Focus your attention on the back of the throat and notice when you breathe this way, there is an openness in your throat that makes the passing breath sound much like the ocean!

Now, keep the same breathing going in your open throat except close your mouth. The air comes in and out of your nose, but still takes the same pathway down and up your throat. Repeat for 5 -10 breaths. This helps release brain and body chemicals that tend to induce sleep.

Sitting is the new smoking, and it's not just the kids that are sitting too much! We must keep regular exercise as a part of our self-care to extend life and stimulate peak performance. We're not going to tell you to go to the gym. We support the idea, but you already know you need some form of regular physical activity and assume you are already doing it.

We're going to suggest something else, something that involves movement, a form of meditating *while* moving.

Here's another mindfulness exercise taught to us by Wellness Coach Roberta Mittman we've done several times in workshops. This is an exercise you can do once per hour or so, especially when your job requires you to sit focused in front of the computer screen or you've been sitting on the phone for an extended period of time.

(4) To start your **Meditative Walking**, get up and start walking around the room at a normal speed, feeling your body in its movement. Notice your arms swinging, your legs coordinating your movement, your feet making contact with the floor, and your breathing in and out as you walk.

Then glance around the room and identify 3 things that have been there all along, but you hadn't noticed yet today. Take delight in noticing the environment around you that has been there to support you all along. Notice colors or shapes, wallpaper or carpet, objects on desks, or sounds you may have been unaware of before.

Now, consciously take some deep breaths in the following ways:

Inhale as you step forward with your left foot, counting to four with each additional step, as you continue to inhale. You will come back to your left foot on the 5th step. On the 5th step, begin your exhaling for four steps, and return to inhale again on the 9th step. You are inhaling and exhaling for four steps each. Continue this for one minute.

Next, continue the same inhaling procedure for four steps, but on the 5th through 8th steps *hold* that breath. Then exhale on steps 9 through 12. Hold your breath again while you take four more steps. Now you are inhaling for four steps, holding for four steps, exhaling for 4 steps, resting your breathing for 4 steps. Continue with this for one minute.

You can do this no matter what anyone else is doing and without them knowing you are doing it. This will clear, relax, and recharge your mind. [36]

Have fun as you deepen your peace, enhance your energy and keep your balance in the midst of your business adventures!

Endnotes

1   http://www.forbes.com/sites/brucejapsen/2012/09/12/u-s-workforce-illness-costs-576b-annually-from-sick-days-to-workers-compensation

2   Ibid.

3   SHRM report: "Retaining Talent" http://www.shrm.org/about/foundation/research/documents/retaining%20talent-%20final.pdf

4   Anchor, Shawn. TED talks, "The Happiness Advantage", https://www.youtube.com/watch?v=GXy__kBVq1M

5   *A Course in Miracles*, Foundation for Inner Peace

6   From the film, "Legendary Coaches"
7
    http://sports.espn.go.com/ncb/news/story?id=5249709

8   https://blog.kissmetrics.com/zappos-art-of-culture/

9   http://www.personaltransformation.com/bernie_siegel.html. See also Marianne Williamson, Return to Love, p. 230.

10 Spring Forest Qigong Level One class and many other places

11 http://www.callthecoach.com/11.html

12 Medical testimonies at http://www.bornahealer.com

13 Ibid.

14 Vironika Tugaleva, *The Love Mindset*

[15]   Marianne Williamson, Return to Love p 96.

[16]   Wayne Gretzky, from Wikipedia

[17]   http://www.callthecoach.com/7.html

[18]   https://www.goodreads.com/quotes/243081-the-ego-however-is-not-who-you-really-are-the

[19]   Larson, David, Canfield, Jack, et. al., *Stepping Stones to Success*, vol. 6, 2011.

[20]   Maxwell, John C., http://www.goodreads.com/quotes/34690-people-don-t-care-how-much-you-know-until-they-know

[21]   Hsieh, Tony, https://blog.kissmetrics.com/zappos-art-of-culture/

[22]   Anchor, Shawn. TED talks, "The Happiness Advantage", https://www.youtube.com/watch?v=GXy__kBVq1M

[23]http://www.teampedia.net/wiki/index.php?title=Team_Building_and_Teamwork_Quotes

[24]   Dr. Albert Mehrabian, author of Silent Messages, conducted several studies on nonverbal communication. He found that 7% of any message is conveyed through words, 38% through certain vocal elements, and 55% through nonverbal elements (facial expressions, gestures, posture, etc), 1972.

[25]   Larson, David, *How To Stop Your Anxiety Now!*

[26]   See Stephen Karpman, "Fairy Tales and Script Drama Analysis," Transactional Analysis Bulletin 7, no. 26 (April 1968).

[27]   See Brenda Schaeffer's Loving Me, Loving You: Balancing Love and Power in a Co-Dependent

<u>World,</u> 1997. See also David Larson's <u>How to Stop Your Anxiety Now!,</u> 2000.

[28] Lyubromirsky, <u>The How of Happiness,</u> <u>http://10consulting.blogspot.com/2008/02/have-you-got-happiness-habit_29.html</u>

[29] Deaton, Angus, and Kahneman, Daniel, http://businessjournal.gallup.com/content/150671/happiness-is-love-and-75k.aspx   See also Jim Collins', *Good to Great.* "The idea that the structure of executive compensation is a key driver in corporate performance is simply not supported by the data."   p. 10

[30] Shawn Anchor reports.

[31] Source unknown

[32] Researchers found that the meditation group not only had lower stress levels during the multitasking tests but also were able to concentrate longer without being distracted. David Levy at the University of Washington. <u>http://usatoday30.usatoday.com/money/jobcenter/workplace/bruzzese/story/2012-07-08/meditation-helps-your-work/56071024/1</u>

[33] Adapted from Hicks, Esther and Jerry, *Ask and It is Given.*

[34] Ibid.

[35] Roberta Mittman lecture, April 1, 2014

[36] See more breathing techniques in my book, *How To Stop Your Anxiety Now!*

Reader Reflections:

If you're ready to end the drama that drains your revenue and build a culture that blows the top off your previous expectations, visit our webpage for **free gift** that will help accelerate your business profits to new heights.

www.triumphleadership.com

For daily support and inspiration, join our tribe on Facebook, Triumph Leadership Group:

www.facebook.com/triumphleadership

We look forward to connecting with you!

Kate and David   ph. 570-723-1020

Other Books and CDs from David and Kate! *

How To Stop Your Anxiety Now!

Come join the revolution for peace. Time to drop anxiety and stress forever, and replace them with confidence, joy, and inner calm. David packs 30 years of strategies, tools, and keys to mood management into 200 pages of supportive guidance and amusing stories to keep your life on balance from here on out. Sold in 59 countries so far, you don't want to miss these gems of powerful interventions to make your life flow.

Stepping Stones to Success

David joins Deepak Chopra, Jack Canfield, Denis Waitley, and others, to share the latest in making your dreams come true. David emphasizes their Essence Leadership Training Program, designed for transforming workplaces, and communities into arenas of high productivity and positive relationships.

Wide Awake

David and Kate come together to share their insights and encouragement for uncovering and living fully the wonder of who you are. By reading and applying the wisdom offered in *Wide Awake*, there is little doubt your life will change for the better. At three minutes a day, you can change your life. Be prepared to be challenged, loved, enlightened, and compelled to a life that feels better than you could have imagined.

Serenity CD

You receive three of David's strongest meditations that support positive changes in your important life. Each imagery on this CD is 22 minutes in length, with enchanting background music that transforms you in the following three areas: making important decisions, letting go of what is holding you back, and following your reliable guide from within. Play the Serenity meditations over and over again for continued growth and success in your daily life.

* all are available at www.triumphleadership.com